Sketches of a Journey

OCTAVE MIRBEAU

LA

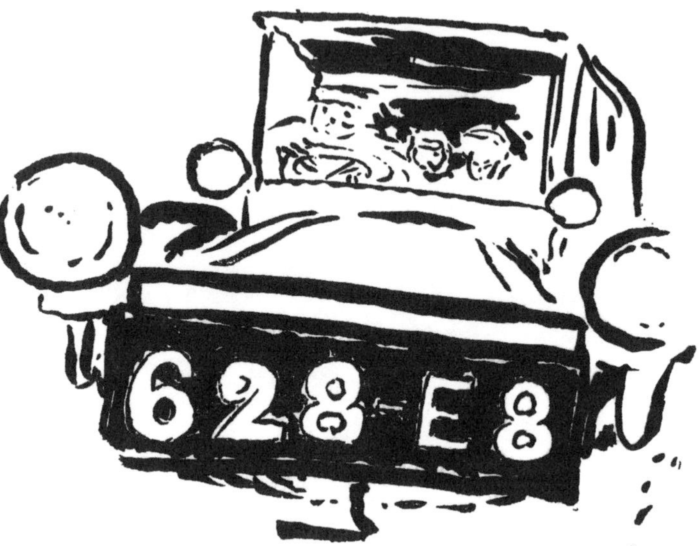

Croquis marginaux de

PIERRE BONNARD

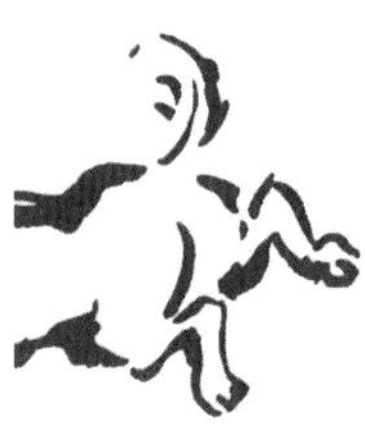

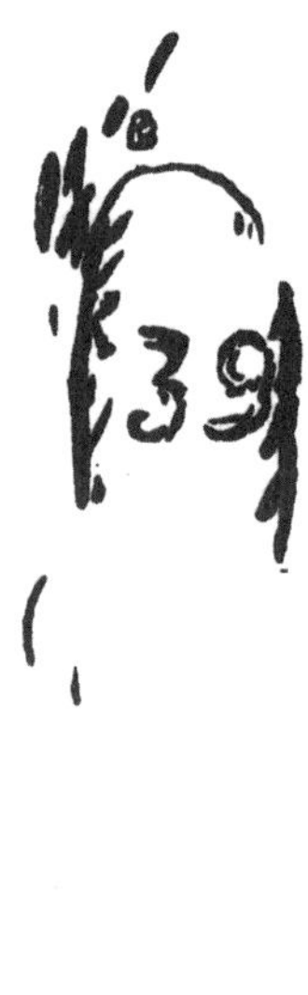

Eugène Fasquelle Éditeur Paris

Bonnard
Sketches of a Journey

Travels in an early motorcar
From Octave Mirbeau's journal 'La 628-E8'
With illustrations by Pierre Bonnard

Philip Wilson Publishers
in association with
Richard Nathanson

Details of future showings of Bonnard's drawings for La 628–E8 can be obtained from:

Richard Nathanson
PO Box 515
London SW15 6LQ
England

First published 1989 by Philip Wilson Publishers Limited
26 Litchfield Street
London WC2H 9NJ

Abridged from the original French book *La 628–E8*, written by Octave Mirbeau and illustrated by Pierre Bonnard.

Distributed in the USA by Harper & Row, Publishers, Inc.
10 East 53rd Street
New York NY 10022

British Library Cataloguing in Publication Data
Mirbeau, Octave
Sketches of a journey
1. Europe, Description & travel, 1900–1914
I. Title II. Nathanson, Richard III. Bonnard, Pierre, *1847–1947*
914'. 04288

ISBN 0 85667 364 1
LC 89-060463

Designed by Roy Cole

Typeset and printed in England by BAS Printers Limited, Over Wallop, Hants. Bound by Dorstel Press Ltd, Harlow, Essex

Foreword

The art of travel is the art of life – for each of us has embarked upon a journey. A journey through which we remain unaware, blissfully and otherwise, of what the next bend will reveal.

And so, too, it is with this journey.

A kaleidoscope of characters and situations unfolds before us. Brossette the chauffeur, the knitting frontier lady, the Belgian waiters, King Leopold, an English lady taking tea, the Kaiser, fig-leafed statues, the giant rabbit of Flanders, horses, hens, ducks and many others, spring from these pages to draw us into their world.

And presiding over this myriad of activity is the magnificent, indomitable and irrepressible
Charron Girardot & Voigt,

A 1904 4-cylinder Charron
(courtesy of Brian Goodman,
photo: Neill Bruce)

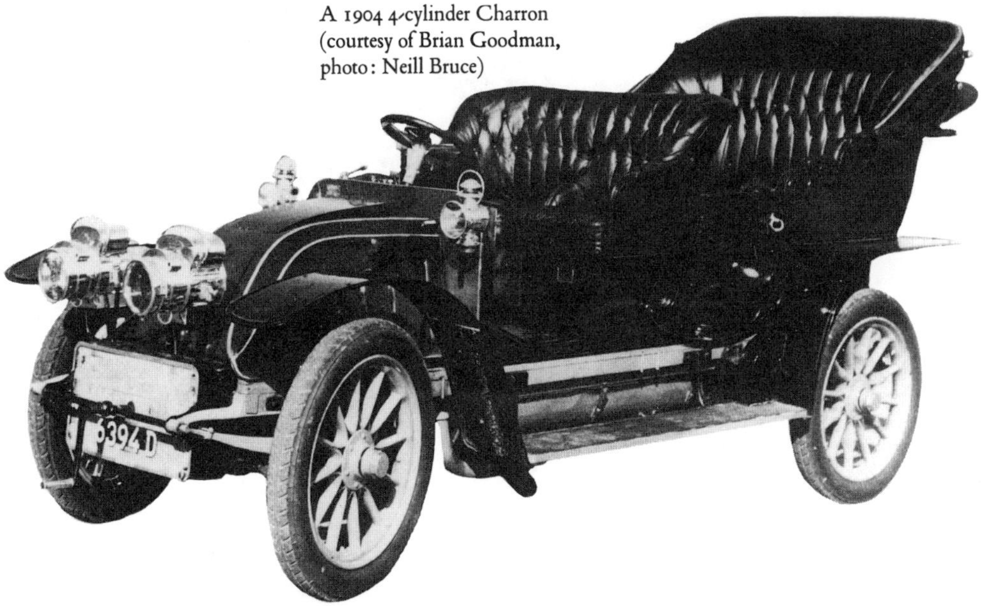

a mouthful for even the French and thus abbreviated to CGV, and known as just – The 628-E8, after its number plate. With a roar and thrust of its engines, The 628-E8 conjures forth event upon event, giving to each a life which, without the magic touch of painter and storyteller, it would not possess.

This is a portrait of life in all its richness, variety, pathos, drama and humorous absurdity. Indeed, as Mirbeau suggests, it is a journey through ourselves.

Mirbeau's journal was first published in France in 1908, and titled 'La 628-E8'. And a special edition, limited to 225 copies, reproduced Bonnard's drawings. Until now, this was the only publication combining the text and drawings. It made no attempt however, visually to integrate the text with the drawings, which were considerably reduced in size and often incomplete.

Sketches of a Journey reproduces the complete set of Bonnard's 104 drawings, for '*La 628-E8*', but it has been designed to allow each drawing to breathe. Mirbeau's text is also translated into English for the first time, but not in full. For now the roles are reversed, and it is Mirbeau who in one sense provides the captions to Bonnard's drawings.

Bonnard met Mirbeau through Thadée Natanson, the art collector and publisher of the famous art journal, *La Revue Blanche*. And '*La 628-E8*' was born out of a deep friendship between writer and painter and their mutual passion for motoring.

'I was very fond of Mirbeau', wrote Bonnard, 'although we had completely different characters, opposite even, I would say. I was first involved with him in his account of a journey of the Low Countries. He had just purchased his first motor car, The 628-E8, and chose his number plate for the title. I made a whole series of drawings for the margins. This amused me very much, for I appreciated Mirbeau's humour enormously. And the whole book is filled with it.'

Octave Mirbeau (1848–1917) was passionate, eccentric, fearless, impulsive, and fused with an enormous energy and appetite for life – a character larger than life. Novelist, playwright, art critic, traveller, businessman, horticulturist, Sunday painter, art collector and raconteur, Mirbeau succeeded at whatever he turned his hand to. He was a loyal friend, and on intimate terms with many of the leading French figures of his day. He championed many causes artistic, literary, social and political, and his early legal training served him well in the courtroom.

He wrote some of the most perceptive catalogue forewords to important exhibitions by the major artists of the period, among them Cézanne, Van Gogh, Gauguin, Renoir, Rodin and Pissarro, and he purchased their work when they were still making their way. Mirbeau was a pivotal force at that particular moment of French genius. And his own novels and plays (listed in the glossary) reflect a highly individual blend of realism, fantasy, poetry and humour, expressed with a painter's eye. Like Bonnard he sought happiness and repose in nature, observing that 'Nature is a strange magician, a perpetual creator of dreams, and a tireless renewer of the ideal – the untarnished source from which we can take all emotions and all miracles'.

The 628-E8 is Mirbeau's heroine, and the vehicle through which his rich, varied and combustous nature, with its deep rooted humanity, is given full vent.

Pierre Bonnard (1867–1947) did not accompany Mirbeau on his more prolonged travels, but he was inspired by the spirit of Mirbeau's account, and by the trip he himself made in 1906 with Misia Natanson, Thadée's wife, along the waterways of Belgium and Holland and down the Rhine. Wherever he went, Bonnard recorded his impressions. He too was a fervent motorcar enthusiast, acquiring in 1911 an 11 CV Renault, which he drove with memorable recklessness.

But from where did this spirit we call Bonnard come? To which school does he belong? And how do we begin to analyse his influences, technique, and all the other paraphernalia which grind down the imagination, and take us further and further from the truth?

Anyone who is moved to pleasure and well-being by Bonnard's art, happily leaves these preoccupations far behind. For Bonnard's joy and wonder at the beauty around him, and his humanity, seize eye and soul, transporting them to an inner kingdom.

Bonnard is French to his core. His theme is the beauty of human beings, Nature, and the home. He is a kindred spirit to Renoir. But this is to do both a gross

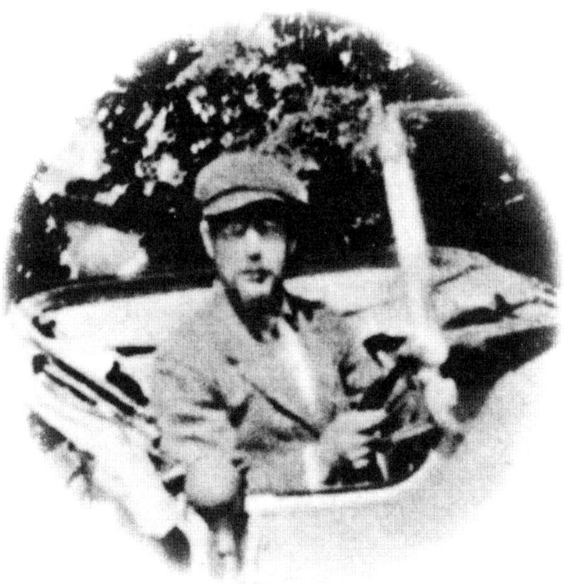

Bonnard at the wheel of his first car in 1912

injustice and say nothing of what it is that makes each unique.

Let us for a moment – for longer would detract from their magic – consider these drawings. As a group they are unique in Bonnard's work, both for their unifying theme and humour, and for their range of subject which touches upon virtually every aspect of Bonnard's work. Their seemingly childlike simplicity and freedom are deceptive. The ability to express humour and pathos in a line comes only from tremendous insight and passion. Their theme – Life – belongs to us all. But it is given to very few, to convey Life's elements in so direct and universal a way.

Following the fracas with the French customs, readers will be brought to an even more abrupt halt by a list at the end of the book, (by no means complete) of publications of Bonnard's work. But among the many books on Bonnard, this journey stands alone, for it is both by Bonnard and about him. It is not a catalogue of drawings, but an idea about life, which Bonnard chose to illustrate and make his own. It brings into play all his imagery, his love of people and Nature, and an artistry which continues until the last perfectly controlled caress of a single brush hair.

The drawings that Bonnard made with such enthusiasm and affection for Mirbeau, underline the creative potential of a harmonious association between artist and writer. They brilliantly illustrate Mirbeau's text providing a subtle foil to his often acerbic wit. And they offer fresh insight into Bonnard's quiet and gentle genius. Perhaps because '*La 628-E8*' was also a symbol of wealth, power, progress and thus the dilemma of our age, Bonnard's drawings pass beyond the immediate and into a timeless world of their own.

The car is a feature of our everyday life. But compare the quality of the journeys we make, with The 628-E8's perambulating sense of adventure and enjoyment.

'*La 628-E8*' was the only motoring book ever to be illustrated throughout by a very great artist. And if something of the art of observing and experiencing portrayed in these pages, could enter our own journeys, however long or local, then Bonnard and Mirbeau will have accomplished all that they set out to achieve. But perhaps the greatest tribute will be the touching enchantment they will bring to both young and old, to Bonnard scholars, and to many who will be seeing Bonnard and reading Mirbeau for the very first time.

Richard Nathanson

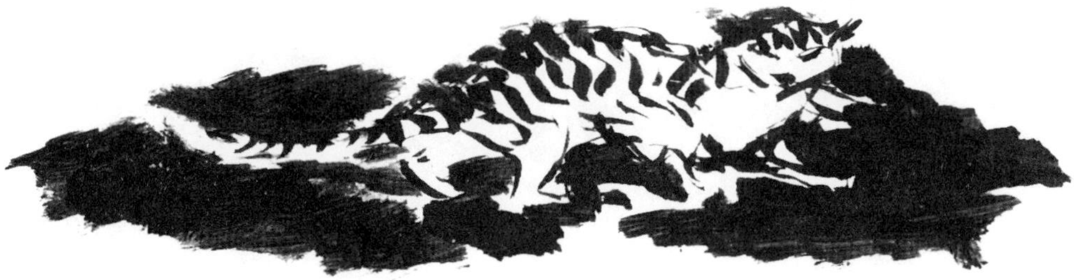

To Monsieur Fernand Charron

To whom should I dedicate the account of this journey if not you, dear Monsieur Charron, who has designed, built and breathed life into this marvellous motor car making it possible, without the slightest fatigue or hint of trouble?

I owe you this tribute in return for many delights, new experiences, and a wealth of precious knowledge which no books could have furnished; and for month upon month of perfect freedom, away from humdrum worries and greater cares; a holiday, indeed, from myself. New places, new people and new impressions of our own and other countries.

Octave Mirbeau

Departure

Here, then, is the journal of a motor tour through parts of France, Belgium, Holland and Germany; and, more especially, through a small part of myself.

Yet is it really a journal? Is it even a tour?

Perhaps it is simply a tissue of daydreams, memories, impressions and stories that have nothing to do with the countries visited, but simply brought to mind by the recollection of a face, a passing landscape, a half-heard voice singing or weeping on the wind. But am I certain that I really heard such a voice or genuinely saw the face which brought back so many memories, both joyous and

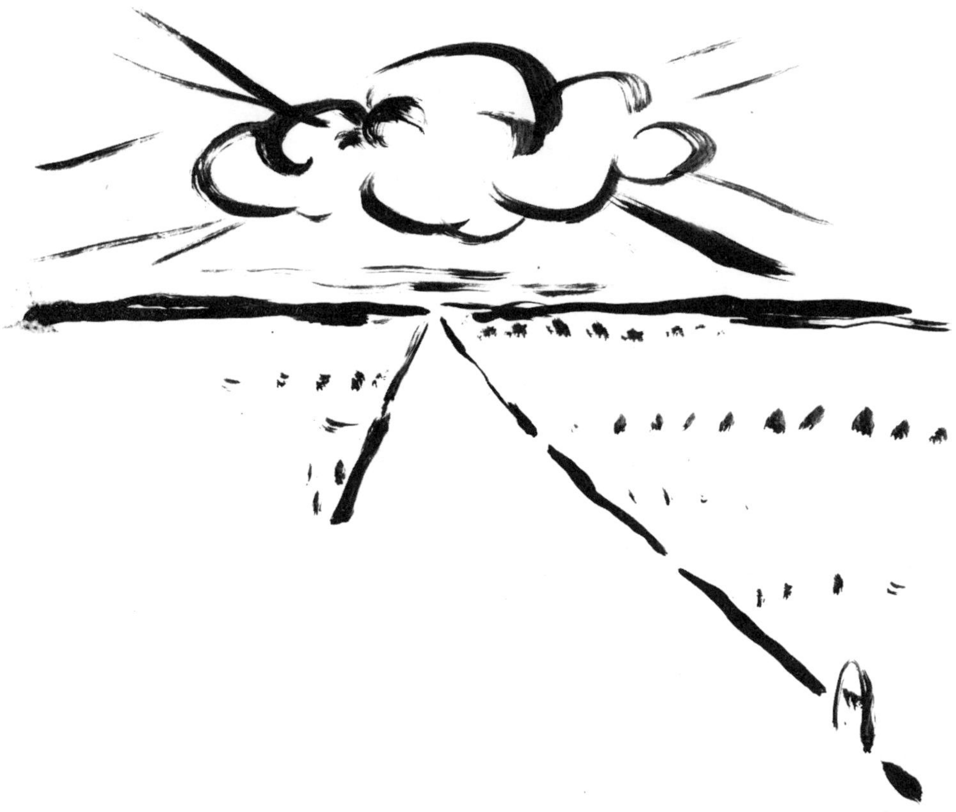

sad; and that I truly glimpsed the landscapes which inspired the rough poetry of the following pages?

There are moments when I ask myself seriously which part of this is the dream and which the reality. I just do not know. Motoring has such a bewildering effect that one cannot be sure. The motor car is all whim and fancy; it engenders incoherence, forgetfulness. You set out for Bordeaux and that evening you are in Lille. But Lille or Bordeaux, Florence or Berlin, Budapest, Madrid, Montpellier or Pontarlier – what difference does it make?

The speed of travel confuses impressions, batters the mind and upsets one's balance. When you get out of the car after a twelve-hour drive, you feel like a patient recovering from a fainting fit who gradually resumes contact with the outside world. Objects are distorted and refuse to stand still. Your ears hum as though assailed by hordes of buzzing insects. With an effort, your eyelids blink open to reality, like a curtain slowly rising to reveal a stage set. So what has been happening? You retain only the vaguest impression of empty spaces, of an infinite whiteness lit by innumerable tiny tongues of fire. You have to shake and pinch yourself to make sure there is solid ground underneath, that you are surrounded by buildings, by people talking and going about their business. Only later in the evening, after dinner, do you really come to. Even then you still feel somewhat restless and uneasy, and these sensations return, more violently than ever, to trouble your dreams.

So, if you ask me whether this is going to be the journal of a neurotic, a madman, all I can reply is that few of us can boast of being entirely healthy and sane.

I know travellers who have a habit of jotting down their impressions of daily events as they go. They drift through

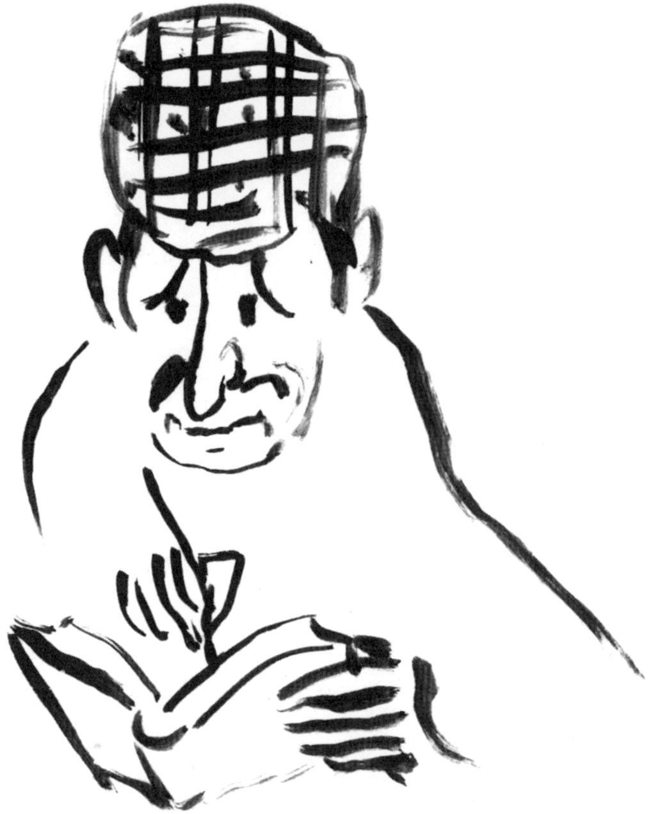

museums and art
galleries, pen in one hand,
notebook in the other, Baedeker in
their pocket, with distracted eyes and vacant
minds. They will stop at some historic ruin, recommended beauty spot or ancient battlefield, and make a note of their 'ideas and sensations', which are usually no more than echoes of something read the previous day. Nor will they go to sleep before scrupulously recording their experiences – and their out-of-pocket expenses.

I found this, for example, in a tourist's notebook left behind in a hotel:

> 'Did the Château of Chambord (see description in Baedeker). They don't build places like that any more. A change from all the horrors of the present day (leftist politicans, strikes, etc.). Spent the entire day among the noble glories of the past (François I, Diane de Poitiers, duchesse d'Etampes). Feel reborn, and what is more (expand this). Gave the guide 2 francs, which wife says is too much. Bought picture postcards (60 centimes) – which shows how they put up the cost of a holiday nowadays.'

I admire people like that. Perhaps they are party to joys I can never share. In any case, I prefer my own, which, for all I know, may not be joys at all.

So I shall simply jot down my recollections and my dreams just as they come into my head, without trying to sort them out.

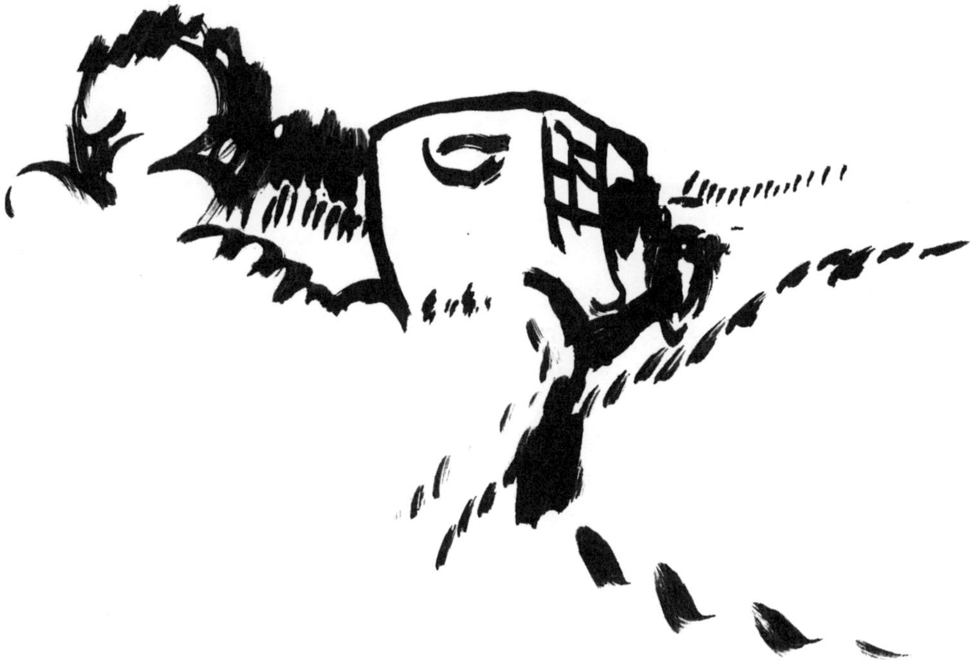

Speed

Motoring, it must be admitted, is a disease, a sickness of the mind. And it has a very pretty name – *la vitesse.* Have you noticed how illnesses nearly always have charming names? Scarlatina, angina, pneumonia, beri-beri, impetigo . . . . And the nicer the name the more serious the disease. I revel in repeating ours: *la vitesse.* Not the mechanical motion that carries the car along roads and across frontiers, but the quality of speed itself – you could call it neuropathic – which animates all the motorist's actions. He cannot keep still – quivering, nerves taut as springs, impatient to be off again the moment he arrives, in agony to be somewhere – anywhere – else. His brain is a racetrack around which jumbled thoughts and sensations roar past at 60 miles an hour, always at full throttle. Speed governs his life: he drives like the wind, thinks like the wind, makes love like the wind, lives a whirlwind existence. Life comes hurtling at him and buffeting him from every direction, as in a mad cavalry charge, only to melt flickeringly away like a film or like the trees, hedges and walls that line the road. Everything around him, and inside him, dances, leaps and gallops, in inverse proportion to his own movement; not always a pleasant sensation, but powerful, delirious and intoxicating, like vertigo or fever.

Suppose I decide to revisit Amsterdam. I make up my mind to stay there a week, a week of oblivion, a week of fun. I need a week merely to skim the surface of that admirable city. If that's not enough I'll take a fortnight. I am free, with all the time in the world. Nothing to keep me here, and absolutely no hurry there.

So off I go.

And here I am again in Amsterdam – somewhat exhausted after the battering the car has received from the appalling Belgian roads – but glad to be back. One week, two weeks, say. Not enough. Let's make it three. I explain this to my chauffeur.

'Brossette, we shall be staying here a month, maybe longer.'

'Very good, sir', he grins. 'Then you'll be wanting all the luggage brought in?'

'Yes, the lot . . . I suppose.'

'Very good, sir.'

'And look, Brossette. I shan't be wanting the car while we are here. Take some time off.'

'Very good, sir.' His grin broadens. 'I'll come round this evening for orders anyway.'

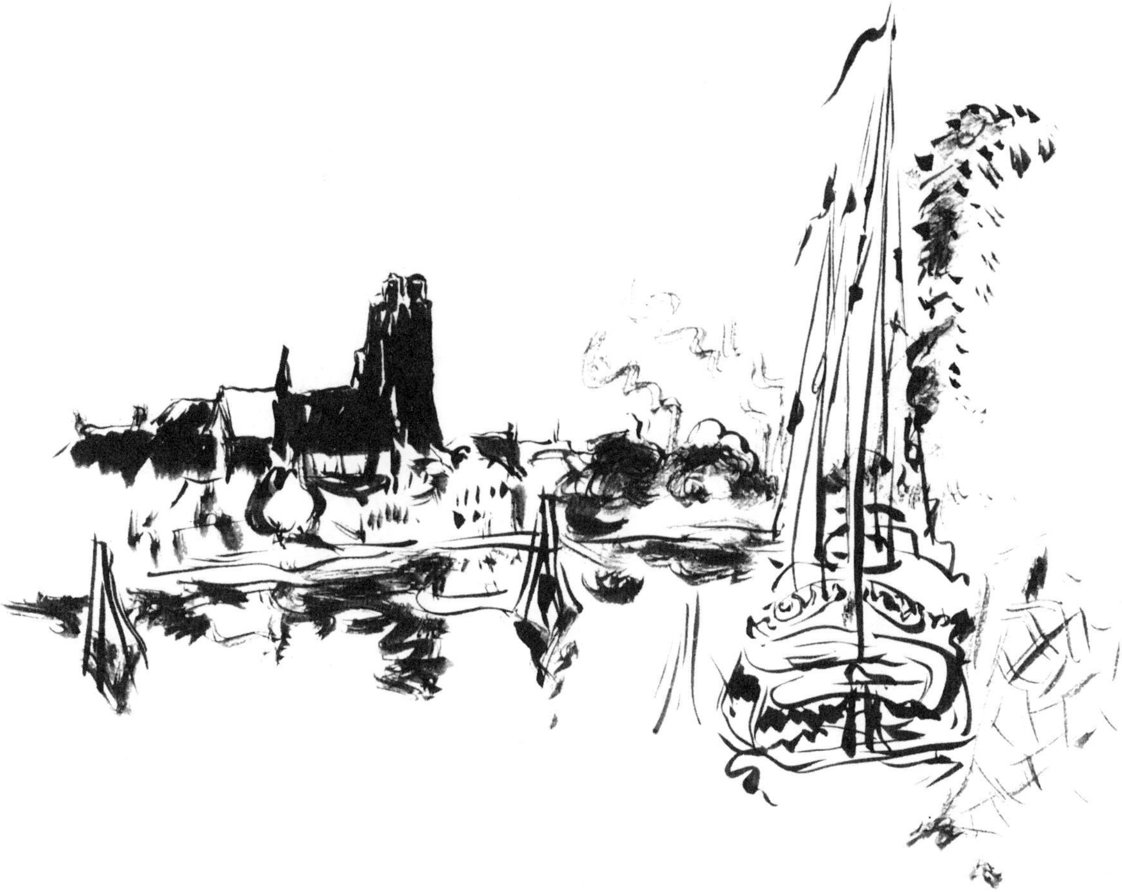

'No, no, certainly not. Go to bed. Go out and enjoy yourself.'

He puts the car away.

I go straight upstairs, take a shower and rub myself down with essence of sage and rosemary. Refreshed and relaxed, I head into town. I step out with springy, confident strides. My footsteps beat a tattoo on the pavement. For no particular reason I find myself running . . . .

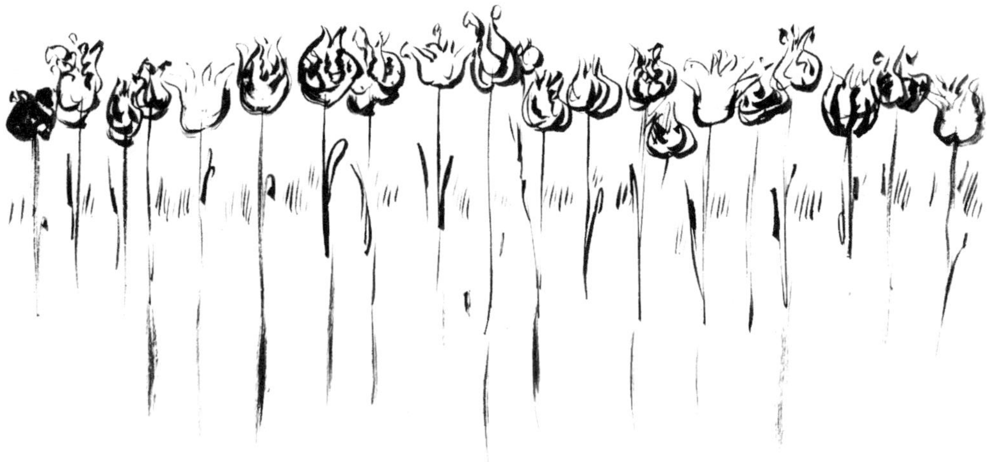

Let's start with the museums. Those marvellous museums where the genius of Rembrandt and Vermeer takes away the taste of Paris *Expositions* and the mawkish whimsies of *l'art nouveau*; an endless procession of galleries in which I seem to be standing still while the pictures flash past in a blur so rapidly that I can hardly tell one from another.

Next moment, not knowing how or why, I am walking beside the canals, their surface glazed, metallic and still, broken only as stately Dutch barges, like Chinese junks, glide past, the mordant greens of their broad prows reflected in the dark waters.

Now I am in the residential quarter, with its crisscross of squares, streets and lanes, with colour everywhere, on the tall narrow façades of houses that huddle together so tightly that they almost suffocate one another. Twice, three times I have crossed the Dam. On and on I walk, every shop window reflecting the image of a frantically scurrying figure – myself.

I continue through gardens with masses of tulips, past huge brick buildings, banks like fortresses, the red bulk of the stock exchange, more canals, more bridges, more houses, dancing and dissolving in the water; and there, a stone's throw from the Kalverstraat, is the little Catholic convent, silent and invisible, quite lost among the busy, bustling shops, its tiny church and narrow triangular gardens, sadly lacking greenery or flowers, its small green-gabled buildings with old, old women in flat coifs squatting outside, praying and swaying their heads and never looking at you, never looking at anything, and who have never looked at anything, ever.

I walk on and arrive at the docks.

Evening falls, and with it comes a damp and biting wind. Through the mist I can see nothing save dim red, yellow and green lamps casting an intermittent light over the canal. Foghorns wail continuously, like lost dogs in the night. Then I plunge on into the little-known waterfront district, a slum of noisy, sleazy dance-halls; a strange, muddy, frozen land of the Indies, part northern, part Javanese, whose inhabitants hold high carnival with shrill oriental music that sets the nerves on edge. The smell, too, grips one by the throat, a mixture of sea air, tar, raw spirits, opium, paraffin and unwashed humanity of every hue, with here and there a gleam of gold encircling a raised arm or high-kicking ankle . . . and other sights besides.

But I don't stop. I fend off the clutches of a negress, her thick, betel-stained lips belching lewd invitations in my face, reeking of death. I go on and on, not knowing where I am heading. . . .

Eventually I get back safely to my hotel, exhausted, bewildered, my head splitting with the pressure from so

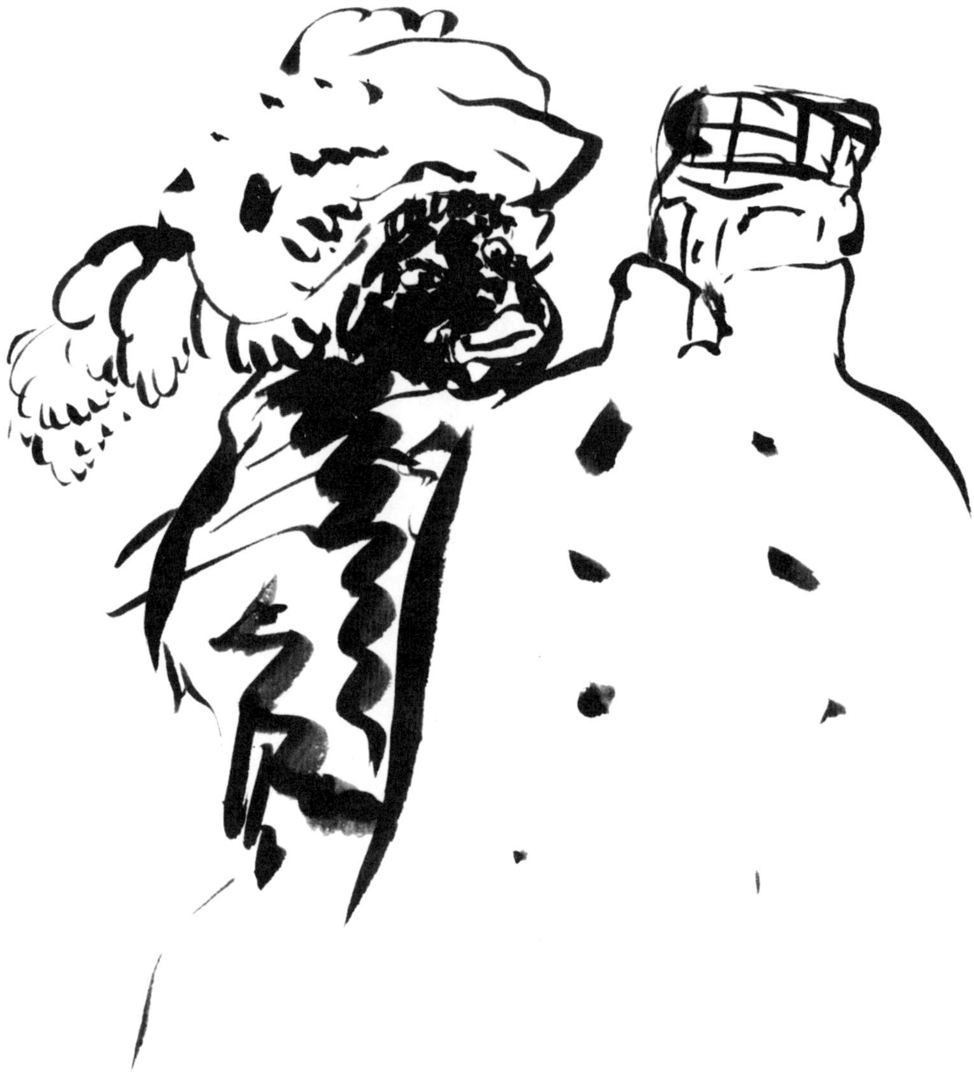

many sundered images clamouring vainly to be made whole. I have only one burning desire; to get away, simply to get away!

Brossette is there waiting for me. He is chatting to the hall-porter. Showing off, miming corners he has taken, breakneck speeds attained and journeys he has never made, when only his coolness, quick thinking and mechanical brilliance have saved me from certain death. I am so delighted to see him that I could almost hug the fellow.

'Hello there, Brossette,' I cry. 'Is the car ready?'

'Yes, sir.'

'Right, then; tomorrow morning, seven o'clock sharp, we'll be off.'

Brossette is not the least bit surprised. He is used to my sudden changes of plan; but he cannot avoid showing, discreetly, of course, that he is pleased. I know that he doesn't like Amsterdam, because one day he grumbled, 'Not much of a place for us chauffeurs . . . .'

He prefers Trouville, Dieppe, Monte Carlo, Ostend – fashionable resorts which cater for motorists. And the place of his dreams is the Avenue de la Grande Armée in Paris.

'So we'll be returning to Paris, sir?'

'Yes, Brossette, back to Paris. In one go.'

'Quite right, too, sir. Forgive me for saying so, but I've no time for places where they serve petrol straight out of the barrel.'

But there you are. I expect he also feels dizzy when he is not in the car, hands on the steering-wheel. Only then is his mind really at peace, like mine.

Brossette is no fool, either. Despite my instructions, the only luggage he had brought in was my overnight bag . . . .

The motor trade

Brossette deserves a chapter to himself, but first a word or two about the natural habitat of this new zoological species: the chauffeur-mechanic.

The motor trade is still on the fringes, with a reputation akin to that of the gambling den and the brothel. In the early days it catered exclusively for the world of wealth and pleasure, attracting seedy aristocrats, penniless playboys, spongers, racing touts, tarts, pimps and all that riff-raff in flowered waistcoats who make a dubious living out of betting and prostitution and conduct their business from their clubs and changing-rooms. These gentry pounced delightedly upon the motor car. The duke of this and viscount that, who formerly scratched a living by pandering to the whims of American millionaires and jumped-up bankers with their fake antique furniture, sham *objets d'art*, dubious paintings and, occasionally, young ladies to sleep with or to marry, began dealing in cars, gracing with their presence (in return for payment, of course) the many garages and showrooms that were springing up everywhere to cater for – or rather exploit – the new clientèle.

These establishments gathered teams of mechanics, giving them rudimentary instruction in driving and motor maintenance. But above all, they taught them subtle ways of tinkering with a vehicle with a view to getting commissions on the sale of one and the purchase of another. They learned ingenious tricks to bump up expenditure on tools and accessories, to cheat on petrol and oil consumption and to exploit the fragility of a pneumatic tyre. It was an amoral school in which teachers and pupils alike soon lost all sense of values, of what their rubbish was really worth. It was crazy. Something that would cost 2 sous anywhere else sold here for 10 francs. I myself got a bill of 100 francs for soldering a headlamp, which should have cost three . . . .

The garages and the mechanics ran no risks, for they could count on the ignorance of the owner who, confronted with a problem, would be met with a barrage of technical jargon: 'But sir, it's the gear-selectors . . . the camshaft . . . the clutch-cone . . . the differential . . . .' And faced with such terrible words, what could he do? He paid. What is more, he even showed pride in boasting to his friends, 'I'm delighted with my car. She runs beautifully. Yesterday I had trouble with the differential . . . .'

Today, when the motor trade is expanding and competition is fierce, conditions are beginning to revert to normal. Garage proprietors seem eager to check the evils they have unleashed, just as successful crooks and ageing courtesans look forward to an honourable retirement. Handouts are no longer given to mechanics on cars brought in for repair, and commission rates are gradually being reduced to a reasonable level. Suddenly the cry is 'Honesty is the best policy – and a clear conscience!'

Whether the employees themselves will really change remains to be seen. After all, those profits, though immoral, raised their standards of living, set them up as a class apart, the envy of other workers. When I discussed the matter one day with Brossette, he remarked, 'Well, so what, sir? The rich can afford it, can't they?'

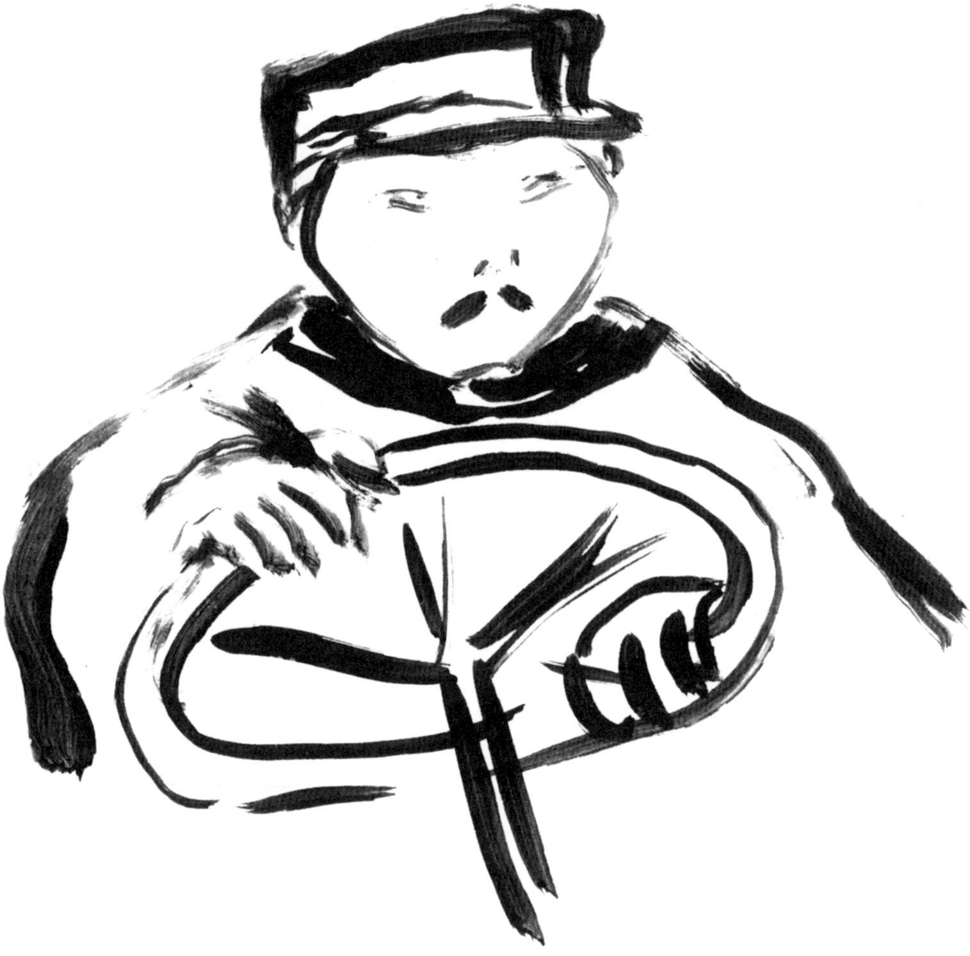

My chauffeur

Brossette – Charles-Louis-Eugène Brossette – was born in Touraine, in a little village near Amboise. Until he was twenty he worked in his father's smithy, where he learned to love horses and 'engineering', the two passions which have dominated his life. While he was away doing military service, his father, one of the most accomplished drunkards in the neighbourhood, died; so young Charles Brossette took service as a carter on a large farm, and then as coachman to a wealthy bourgeois family. He was fond of horses, understood them instinctively, was equally happy on the box and in the stable, but loathed wearing livery. His employers complained that he looked a dreadful sight. He still does.

When cars first came in, Brossette saw his chance. He had saved some money – for despite the laws of heredity he is abstemious and even a bit stingy – and went off to Paris to learn this new trade in a garage. He was bright and good with his hands; and he became obsessed with engines. Soon the country bumpkin was more than a match for the wiliest dealers in Paris. He moved from factory to factory, workshop to workshop, getting to know every make of car. He drove courtesans, financiers and dukes; he went touring, assisted runaway couples and took part in rallies.

When I first met him he was just back from America, somewhat disillusioned, he looking for a car, I for a chauffeur. I asked what he thought of America. 'Nothing to write home about, sir,' he replied. 'A bit like Aubervilliers, but bigger.'

The answer was on the short side, but it amused me, and I took him on.

I had difficulty getting used to him at first. Then he grew on me, like a bad habit.

Brossette is pure motor trade. He can't distinguish too well between what is mine and what is his, and deliberately mistakes my purse for his own. For the past three years, extraordinary to relate, the petrol tank on our car has suffered incessantly from holes, introduced by some diabolic agency, invisible holes through which the fuel leaks away and which have proved impossible to plug. A bad example and contagious to boot, for the neighbouring oil tank suffers from the same complaint.

At the end of each month, when Brossette brings me his book, the same conversation takes place.

'Look here, Brossette, I don't understand. On Tuesday the 17th you've put down 55 litres of petrol . . . .'

'Possibly, sir.'

'Right. Wednesday the 18th another 55 litres.'

'Yes, sir.'

'Very well. But don't you remember? That Wednesday we didn't go out.'

'Of course. But if we had done . . . .'

'And I see that on Thursday the 19th there's another 55 litres . . . .'

'Naturally, sir. That blasted tank . . . .'

'And the oil? You'll never convince me . . . .'

'The sump leaks too. Simple enough. They both leak. It just runs away.'

'Then mend them, for goodness' sake!'

'But I do so all the time, sir. I'm worn out with mending them. I can't do more!'

I hate to point out that the poor chap is a liar and a cheat. These things happen in the best families. I say nothing and fork out.

 Besides, Brossette's good points more than make

up for his professional lapses. He is an excellent travelling companion, amusing, resourceful, attentive without being servile and, apart from his fanciful bookkeeping, utterly loyal. He is fun and I have complete confidence in his driving; he is coolness itself, takes no unnecessary risks but can act decisively if need be. He does not know the meaning of fatigue, and whatever happens always looks on the bright side. The way he deals with gendarmes and cycle cops is marvellous to behold. Thanks to his good humour and charm, we emerge unscathed no matter how strong the evidence against us.

And how he loves that car! He talks about it as he would a pretty woman. Last month we were coming back from Bordeaux after dark. Between Blois and Chartres we 'picked up a puncture' – four times. The other side of Versailles – near Ville d'Avray – a tyre burst for the fifth time. I was irritable and anxious to get home; and I was genuinely sorry for poor Brossette.

'Oh, never mind', I cried. 'Let's drive on as it is!'

He had stopped the car. 'We couldn't do that, sir. It would put too much strain on the differential.' And he set to work, singing to cheer himself up.

Chauffeurs exert a magic on the minds of cooks and housemaids that is almost as irresistible as a soldier's. This magic has noble roots: it stems from the nature of the job, which they regard as heroic and dangerous, just like war itself. A man who launches himself through space like a whirlwind or tornado appears almost superhuman. They remember old prints where angels with long trumpets whip armies into a frenzy, urging them into battle. I think they have much the same idea about chauffeurs.

Even so, Brossette is by no means handsome. He looks far from imposing, certainly not one to conjure up

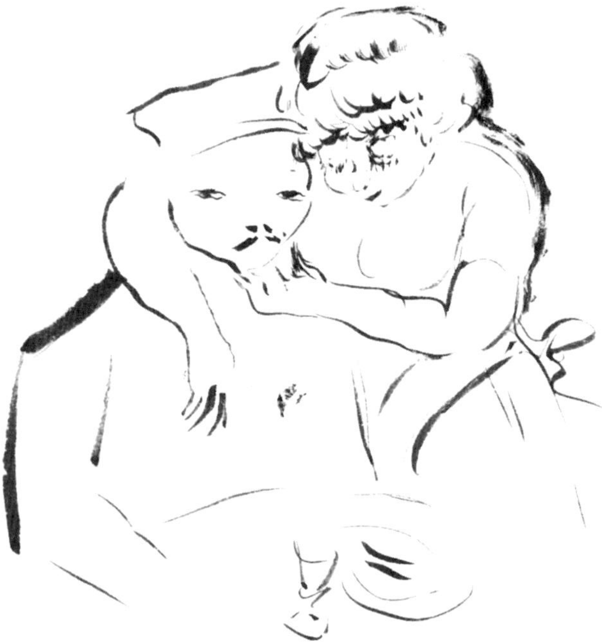

allegories and marvels such as these. He stoops, his chest is flat, his legs are thick and slightly knock-kneed. His little moustache looks as if it were suffering from mange.

Were it not for his rather nice smile, cheerful, mischievous and mocking, his face would offer few inducements to the fair sex. He looks thoroughly untidy, his clothes more often than not torn and grubby. He sticks his cap on the back of his head, and he stumps about like a navvy, hardly the picture of a dashing, romantic lover.

Yet, below stairs, they have no time for anyone else. The cook adores him and the housemaid is crazy about him. They pamper him like a pasha, spoil him like a child. One cooks him special little dishes and crams him with sweets, the other does nothing but press, sew and darn.

They shower him with presents of all sorts, including boxes

of my cigars. He accepts it all with good grace, as a man accustomed to such favours. Always sparing of his energies and strength, Brossette is not a great one for love. He enjoys a bit of occasional horseplay and takes a few liberties. But he leaves it at that.

All this, naturally, gives rise to frightful scenes of jealousy. Often the rivals come to blows, tearing each other's hair out. There is such a banging of pots and pans that in order to settle things I often have to send them both packing, and then it all begins again with the next lot.

I thought, by moving Brossette out of the house, we should have some peace.

'Listen, Brossette,' I said. 'You are quite impossible. You turn everything upside-down. The house is no longer my own. From now on you will find a room and take your meals out.'

He took it quite philosophically. 'A very good idea, sir. At least I shall be able to read *L'Auto* in peace. . . . But look! It won't make any difference, sir. They just don't get on. Cor, these women are a blessed nuisance!'

What I greatly admire about Brossette is his eyesight, so that he can spot obstacles even when we are several miles away; plus his mystifying, uncanny sense of direction. Surprisingly enough, he doesn't boast about this astonishing faculty, he just happens to have it. In pigeons, wild ducks or swallows, an explanation can be attempted, but in Brossette? He sits there hunched, hands barely touching the wheel, scanning the dashboard instruments, glancing at the countryside. Ear attuned to the slightest sound from the engine, he drives on, disregarding the signposts. At a crossroads he raises his head, studies the horizon, sniffs the breeze, then resolutely takes one of the half dozen roads ahead – and it is always the right one.

Crossing the frontier

My friends and I were slightly apprehensive, I admit, when we set out one fine morning in April 1905 in our splendid, powerful and comfortable CGV.

Not very far from Saint-Quentin, where we were paying the customary homage to the pastels of Fantin-Latour, we were pelted with stones; and at La Capelle a couple of gendarmes, waiting in ambush behind glasses of absinthe in a café, stopped us and gruffly demanded to see the car's papers. After an interminable argument, which enabled us once again to admire the smart appearance, careful choice of words and impeccable logic of French officialdom, we received two summonses (despite all Brossette could do), one for exceeding the speed limit, the other because the rear number-plate, 628-E8, was partially obscured by dust. Gendarmes must have something to enliven their dreary vigils in cafés . . . .

As we drove into Givet, a stronghold erected against Belgian invasion, an urchin rolled a heavy log down from a bank, just missing the car and causing a nasty skid.

And this while still in France, sweet France, land of progress, generosity and understanding! How very reassuring! What, wondered my companions, would happen to us in Holland or, worse still, in Germany, where, as is recognised by the most learned historians of *La Patrie*, the primitive creatures who inhabit both countries are no better than savages?

I could say nothing to reassure them. They were not at all happy.

'You are really in for trouble,' they had been told. 'In Holland the Dutchies glare at you like wild beasts,

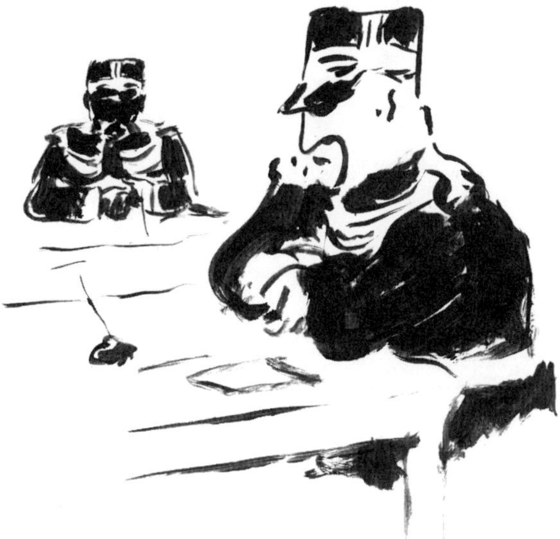

band together in packs and leap on you unawares. Then they'll tip you into the canal. As for Germany, that's even worse. Remember the war of 1870! It doesn't bear thinking what will happen to you. It's terrifying!'

Having been regaled with frightful stories about the hostility of the people, the severity of the regulations, the bloodstained tyranny of the authorities and – not least – the lamentable state of the roads, which were veritable deathtraps, my friends had agreed only after prolonged hesitation to join me. And now we were armed with every possible kind of documentation – political, diplomatic, military and customs – our wallets stuffed with certificates, affidavits and marvellous letters in beautiful handwriting, embellished with impressive red seals. But what good would they all be, when the moment of truth came and we were face to face with barbarians?

The German customs

As it happened, we spent a delightful month in Holland, and at about four o'clock one afternoon, coming from Arnhem, reached Elten. I looked everywhere for the customs post, until finally a cosy little cottage was pointed out. I knocked and called several times, but apparently there was nobody at home. At last I discovered a good lady in one of the rooms placidly darning stockings. She wore large glasses and the expression on her aged face was very sweet. She was stone deaf. At her side lay a ginger cat, curled up on a cushion, fast asleep. An earthenware pot was bubbling away on the hob. I inspected the premises carefully but not a trace could I find of offensive weapons; no racks of rifles, no spiked helmets, not even a picture of Kaiser Wilhelm on the wall. I thought I had come to the wrong place. With great difficulty I made the old dear understand what we wanted.

'Oh yes,' she said, rising heavily from her chair, 'this is the place, to be sure.' She put down her spectacles and her darning upon a table littered with ledgers, papers and forms. The cat awoke and stretched voluptuously.

'Lovely weather for travelling, gentlemen . . . . Now if you will come with me, it's not far . . . .'

We crossed the road and she led me into a bar where a short, fat man, very red in the face, sat smoking a big pipe, with a tankard of beer in front of him. Although he was alone he was chuckling to himself. Perhaps remembering our defeats and *their* victories? After all, what else can the Germans find to think about? The woman murmured something. 'Oh, right,' said the fat man. 'We'll go out and have a look.'

I noticed he was wearing a flat cloth cap jammed

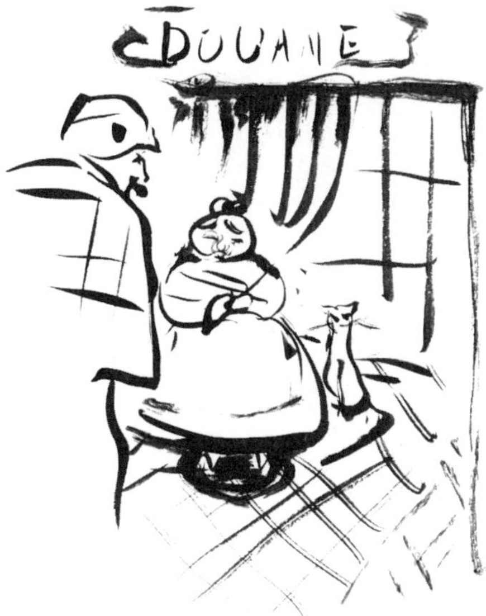

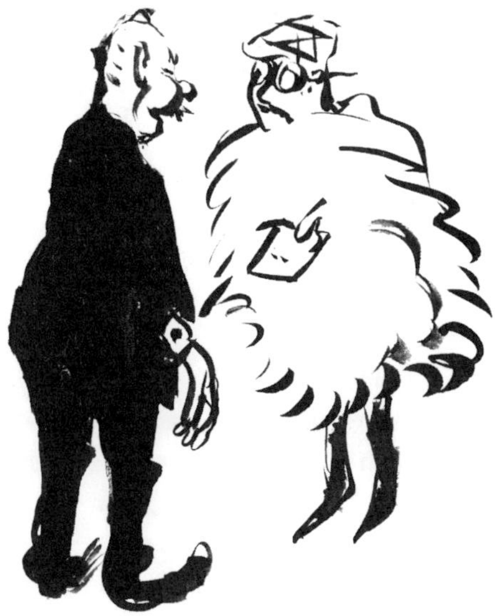

on to his head –
and very funny it looked –
and that his faded garments bore little
resemblance to uniform, save for two or three brass
buttons and the remains of piping here and there. We went
outside.

He walked around the car, examining it with
delighted curiosity. Brossette followed, ready to open trunks

as soon as he was bidden. I drew out my famous wallet full of papers. There then ensued the following dialogue between a French citizen and a German customs official:

'Runs well, eh?'

'Pretty well.'

'Is she fast?'

'Fairly fast, yes.'

'30 kilometres an hour?'

'Oh, more than that. Quite a bit.'

'My, my! She's lovely . . . beautiful!'

He ran his hand over the bulb of the horn, puffed out his cheeks and blew. 'Poop, poop?'

'Yes.'

'That's nice. And you're on your way to Krefeld?'

'No, Düsseldorf. . . .'

'Düsseldorf, eh? Goodness me, then you'd better be off right away. . . .'

He gave me a friendly pat on the shoulder.

'French, eh?'

'Yes.'

He shook me warmly by the hand and pointed down the road. 'Düsseldorf . . . first on the right. At Emmerich you take the ferry across the Rhine. Off you go, now!'

I asked, 'It's a bad road, eh?'

'Bad? It's as smooth as a billiard table? Goodbye!'

Before taking the turn the customs man had indicated, I looked back, and there he was in the middle of the road waving that cap of his to wish us God-speed.

It was some while before we recovered from our astonishment. 'All that must be hiding something pretty awful,' muttered one of the party. 'Keep a good lookout, Brossette. And don't drive so fast!'

And that's how we entered Germany.

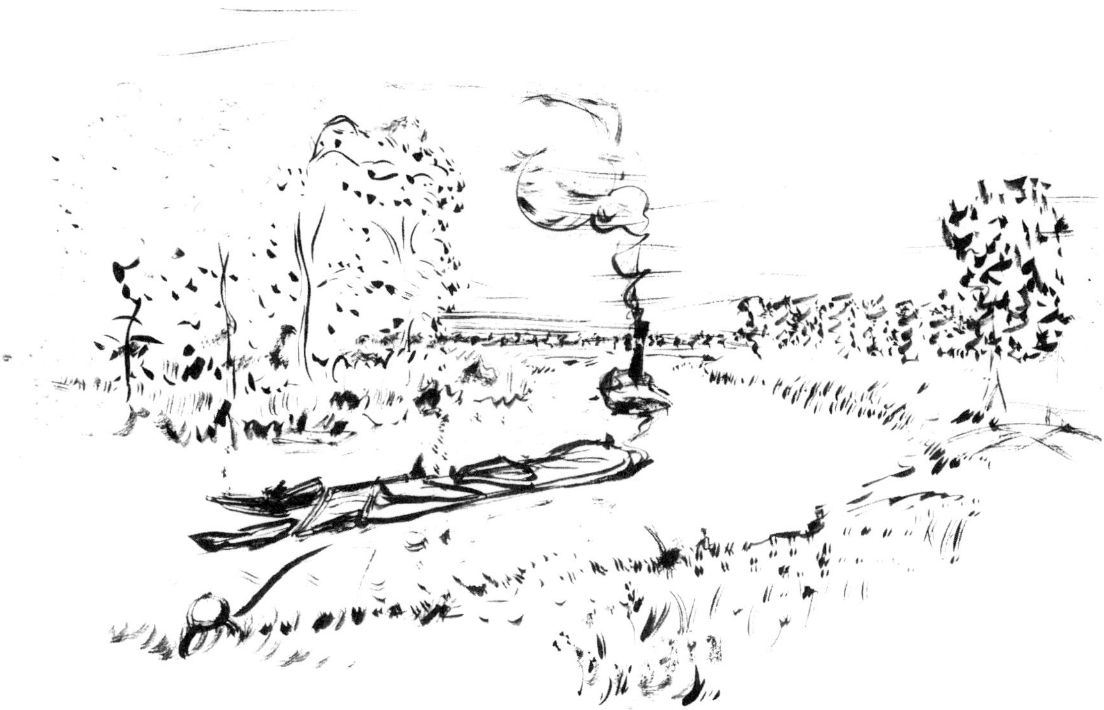

Rocroy – a ghost town

Of course, I'm jumping ahead.
Right now we are bound for Belgium and still heading towards Givet.

First unpleasant day.

After Compiègne the wind freshened, a bleak, chill wind from the north, which slowed us down and blew clouds of dust into our face. So long as we followed the Oise, twisting away from the river and then back again, all went well. The freshness of its valley, the surprise at seeing its charming ports and the movement of its shipping all made a delightful scene. Beyond Saint-Quentin,

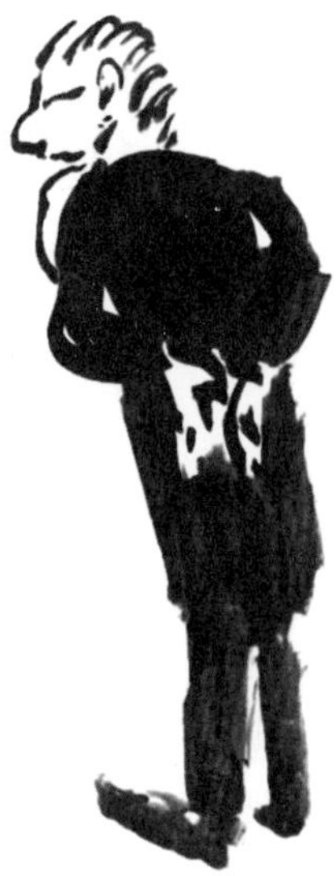

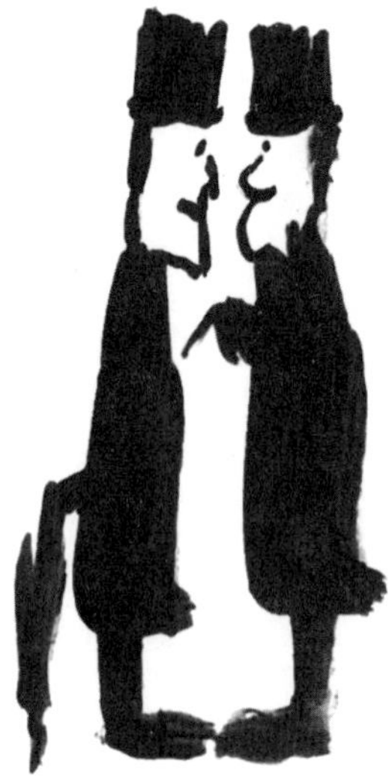

however, the countryside turned
gloomy, and our mood likewise . . . .

We arrived at Rocroy – whose very name resounds with the glories of Louis XIV – by mistake. Against the advice of Brossette, whose instinct is never wrong, I was convinced that this rough, rocky road must be a short cut, and that by taking it we would soon reach Fumay. Alas, it was Rocroy.

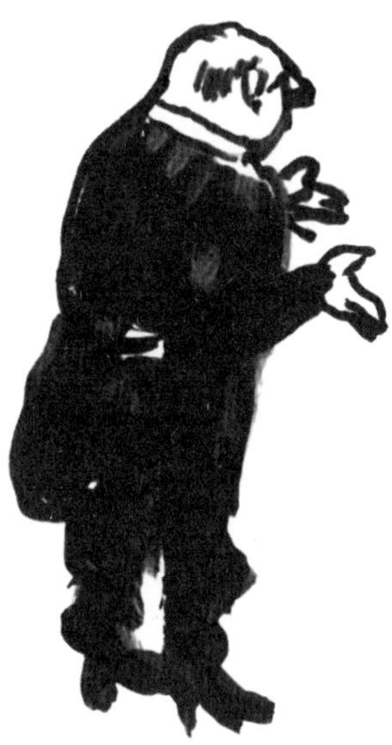

Rocroy retains its ramparts and its two gates. But although built by Vauban, who had both imagination and a sense of the picturesque, they are neither imposing nor decorative. The town consists of little more than a rather miserable, deserted, grubby little square around which huddle buildings of no great age or architectural merit, their walls cracked and stained and peeling like faces attacked by some skin disease. It is all dark, scabby and frighteningly empty . . . . I can't rememeber seeing a tree, a fountain or

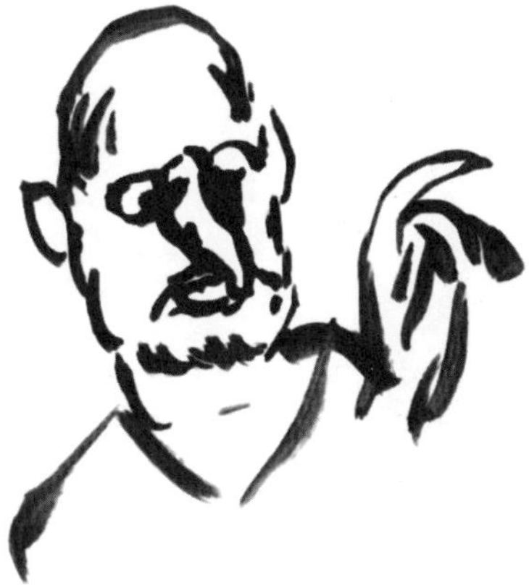

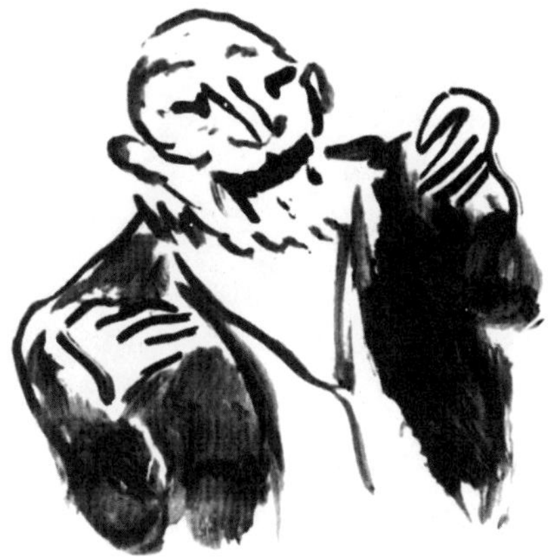

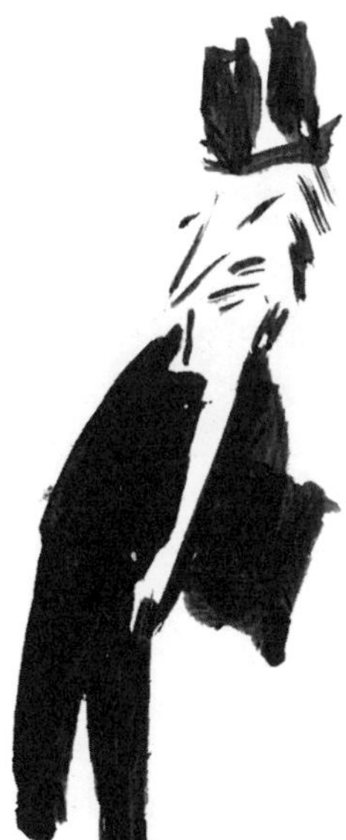

a news-stand. Not a trace anywhere, not even on a shop front or a café sign, of the great Condé . . . .

It was soon evident that this dead ruin was a fair reflection of the destructive political and military policies of Louis XIV, the same disastrous policies that were later pursued by Napoleon and bequeathed to us all. By some miracle France has not died as a result, but the burden remains.

Worthy scholars are today rewriting the history of that abominable century which is generally known as *le grand siècle*. Truly we have no reason to be ashamed of our own, even though we are saddled with the Academies, implacable guardians of yesterday's lies. What are present-day frauds and petty scandals in comparison with the vice and corruption of that famous court which is paraded as the model of integrity, patriotism, elegance and virtue? Those great nobles in their silks and lace were boors and

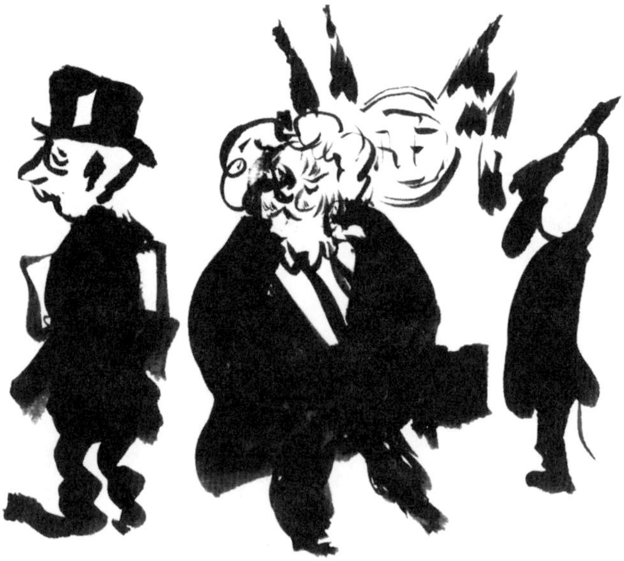

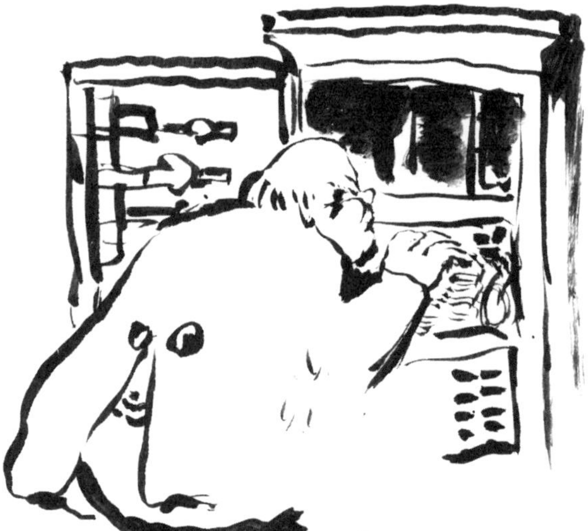

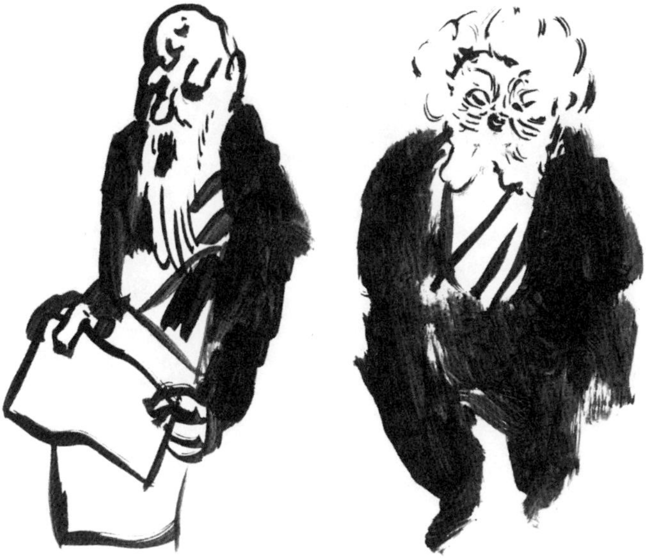

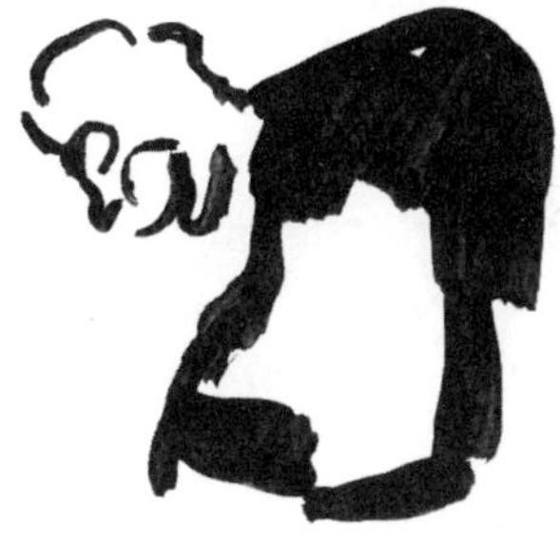

scoundrels to a man, ignorant, thieving pimps and lackeys . . . . Proud upholders of monarchy and religion, they profited from their offices, defrauded the revenue, cheated at cards, betrayed their country, and procured their wives, daughters and mistresses for the King's bed. It was a monstrous, stinking reign, enough to make you feel sick. Neither the beauty of the palaces nor the grace of the gardens and parks, nor the glories of La Rochefoucauld, Pascal, La Bruyère, Corneille, Racine, Molière, Colbert and Saint-Simon can efface the shame and the crimes.

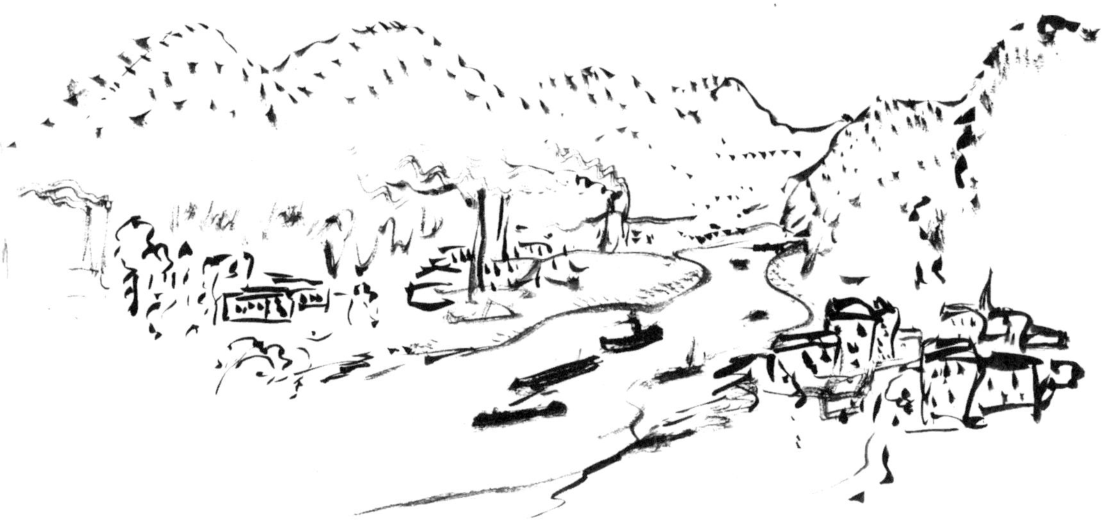

A family of motorists

We spent a reasonably convivial evening in a clean hotel in Givet, where the cuisine was indeed 'simple and modest', siege rations, you might say. The trout from the Meuse on the menu was at the last minute replaced by a humbler fried roach, and they gave us cold meat instead of the promised roast beef; but it was all done so charmingly that we thoroughly enjoyed our dinner.

There was a family – father, mother, daughter and son – at the next table. They had arrived ahead of us and were also travelling by car. But they had been stranded with all kinds of trouble in various outlandish spots, and sounded very cross. The mother, in particular, was complaining bitterly about their car.

'No, there's nothing wrong with her, nothing,' protested the father. 'Just a bit lazy. She'll warm up.'

Mama ignored him. 'I told you we should have bought a Charron like the Levasseurs', or a Panhard like the Tripiers'. They're no fools, that lot! It's marvellous, I must say, to keep breaking down all the time!'

'She'll warm up – just give her time. I mean, be reasonable. It's like buying new shoes; they're never comfortable until you've worn them for a week. You women! You want the moon right away!'

'Well, I know one thing: we'll never get to Brussels in that heap of junk!'

Papa gave a loud guffaw and looked in our direction, as if inviting our opinion. 'Heap of junk, indeed! A Brulard-Taponnier 12 hp .... Very funny!'

'You'll see, you'll see!'

She was flabby, blotchy, affected and bad-tempered; and to prove she had come by car she still had her hideous goggles on, pushed up over her beige felt hat. Her husband was short and fat, with a cheerful round face and little pointed beard, proudly sporting a yachting cap with *Le Touring* badges. The daughter was a graceless, unhealthy-looking girl with ears that stuck out, thin, mousy hair and bad teeth. And as for the son, with his low forehead, sallow complexion and receding chin, he looked a complete moron .... The typical French family, in fact.

They were on their way to Belgium, and never having been out of France before, the prospect of crossing the frontier was worrying them considerably. After dinner, papa had a long talk with the landlord about local industries, mama played patience, the girl leafed idly through Baedeker and the boy fell fast asleep with his mouth open.

Suddenly the girl cried, 'Mother, what's the Manneken-Pis?'

'Hold your tongue, child!' hissed mama, glancing,

uneasily at us. 'How dare you mention such things, you wretched girl!'

'What things?' insisted the daughter, in all innocence. 'Anyway, it's here in Baedeker.'

'It's not a proper subject, so there!'

'Why?'

'Because.'

'Shan't we be seeing the Manneken-Pis, then?'

'Yes, you will see it, but with your mama. Now be quiet!'

Later we were interrupted by their chauffeur, still in his overalls, hands black with grease.

'Ah, Ferdinand, how's the car, eh? Everything all right? We'll be off in the morning at eight o'clock sharp, my lad. Mind you fill up with petrol. Let's see . . . . From here to Namur is roughly 60 kilometres. Just put in enough to get us there.'

The chauffeur looked embarrassed and scratched his head. 'Trouble is, sir . . . well, the car won't go. The clutch won't engage.'

'Goodness . . . nothing serious, I hope?'

'Well, sir, it's a proper nuisance . . . .'

The whole family stared at the poor chap.

'What's that you say? A brand new car?'

'Yes, well . . . . You must understand, sir, if the clutch won't engage . . . .'

'Of course I understand, but that's no reason, surely . . . . Go and get on with it.'

'Well but it's too dark now, sir. I'll have another look in the morning. But I'm afraid . . . .'

And amid much confusion and argument, we crept off to bed.

 Next day in the hotel yard, we witnessed a tragic scene.

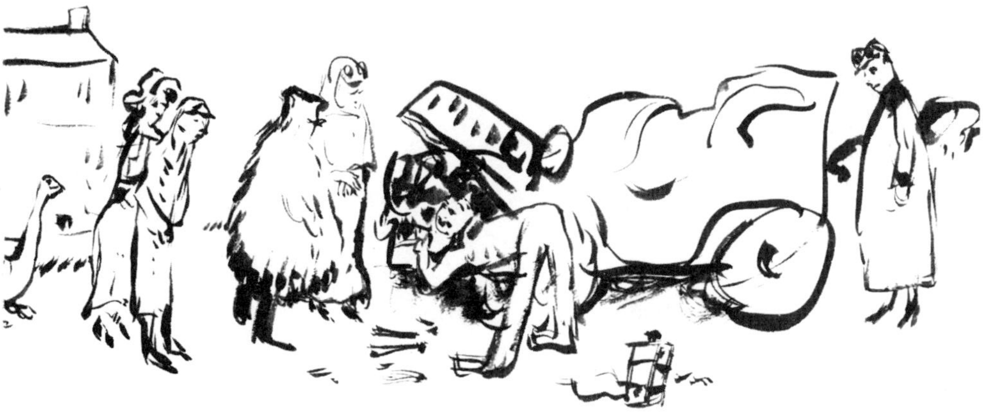

The family, all wrapped up in their motoring clothes, were gathered round the car. We arrived just as Brossette, who had been called in by his colleague for advice, crawled out from under the chassis.

'Well?' demanded the owner.

'Nothing doing,' replied Brossette, dusting himself off. 'The cone's out of alignment, the leather's scorched. It'll have to go back to the works.'

Ferdinand cut in, an enigmatic expression on his face. 'I did say last night, sir . . . . I'll take the blinking car back to Paris, and meet you in Belgium, sir. It's a bit of bad luck, all right. You'll be taking the train . . . repairs will take a week or so. Unless you care to stay here, sir. Naturally, that's up to you, sir.'

'There are some lovely walks in the neighbourhood,' volunteered the landlord, who had been prowling around the car. 'Good horses for hire, comfortable carriages, moderate terms. . . .'

There was a pause. 'Are you sure, Ferdinand, isn't there some way?' the owner implored.

'Ask my colleague, sir!'

Brossette, who was washing his hands at the pump, glanced over his shoulder. 'Nothing to be done. . . .'

Ferdinand shut the bonnet. They all looked at it, as if expecting a miracle, but the engine remained silent.

Mama pursed her lips. The blotches, visible through her veil, turned darker than ever. 'So that's it, then. Isn't she something, your Brulard-Taponnier 12 hp? Isn't she a peach?'

Her husband stood in a daze. He heaved a deep sigh. 'To arrive in Brussels by rail. That's just terrible!'

Brossette had started up the CGV. The daughter had tears in her eyes. Goodbye, perhaps forever, little Manneken-Pis.

Hearing the soft, regular purr of our engine, the poor motorist plucked up courage to say, 'You're lucky. You are certainly lucky.'

'Monsieur has a good car,' his wife corrected him. 'Monsieur doesn't have a Brulard-Taponnier 12 hp!'

Our 628-E8 accelerated away from the hotel at a rate that Brossette deliberately made spectacular.

'Poor souls,' I remarked to Brossette when we were clear of the town.

He was silent for a moment, then shrugged his shoulders and grinned, 'Right mugs, sir. Nothing at all wrong with the car, actually. Just that Ferdinand is suspicious of his wife . . . worried to death. Wants to get home and surprise her. And since they haven't a clue about cars . . . .'

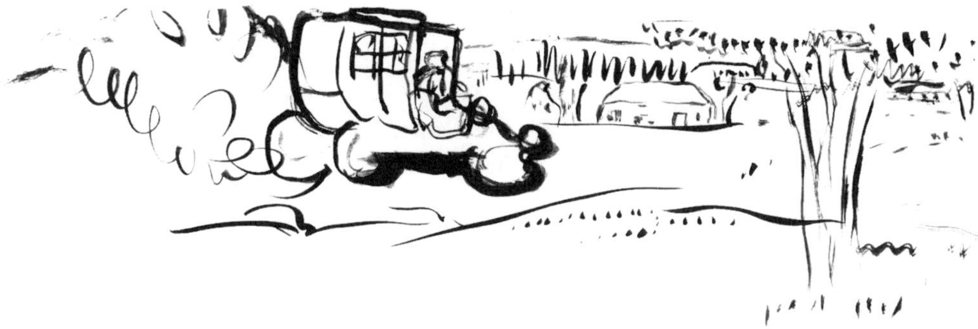

I ticked him off severely
for being party to such a dirty trick.

'Oh, sure, Ferdinand was wrong. Shouldn't have done it. Better to be a cuckold. I told him so, but he wouldn't listen. Still, I couldn't let a pal down. Besides, we're not idiots like that lot!

The air tingled. It was a glorious morning, full of scents. A large boat made its way up the Meuse. We drove fairly fast. Gradually my anger subsided, and by the time we reached the customs the wicked instincts that nag every motorist had got the upper hand. And it was with a certain malicious and quite reprehensible pleasure that I imagined myself back in the hotel yard, the forlorn family still grouped around the silent car, and the landlord doubtless still repeating, 'There are some lovely walks in the neighbourhood. . . .'

Brussels

It really is maddening to have driven from the frontier over those ghastly stones – wave upon wave of them – through the grimy mining country of the Borinage, and to end up in Brussels, this absolute travesty of a town. Brussels is really awful, but here I am, and here I intend to stay, if only to let my ribs and back recover from the bruising they received on those dreadful roads.

In the days of its glory, when the Dukes of Burgundy held court here in barbaric luxury and splendour, when infantas and archdukes ruled it on behalf of the Emperor or King of Spain, Brussels was a city sparkling with cloth of gold, velvet, silks and furs, a city of love and lace, of poetry and sensuality. It was the capital of good living and good drinking, where the privileged and the well-to-do went singing and shouting and staggering through the narrow streets with their
bawdy female companions,

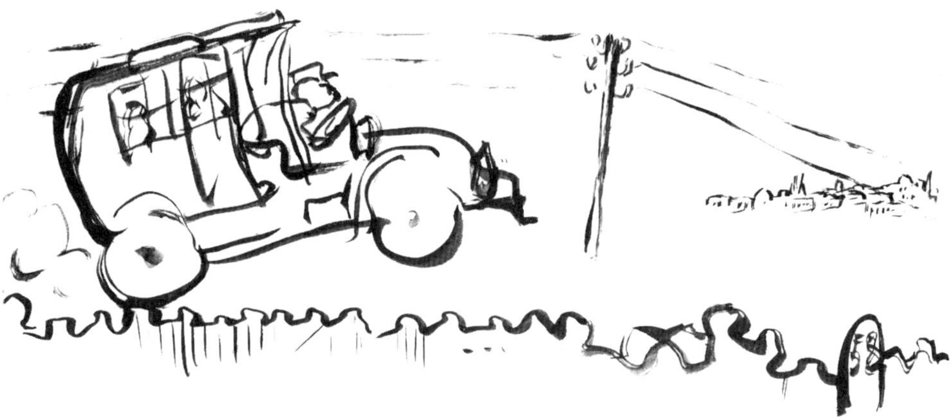

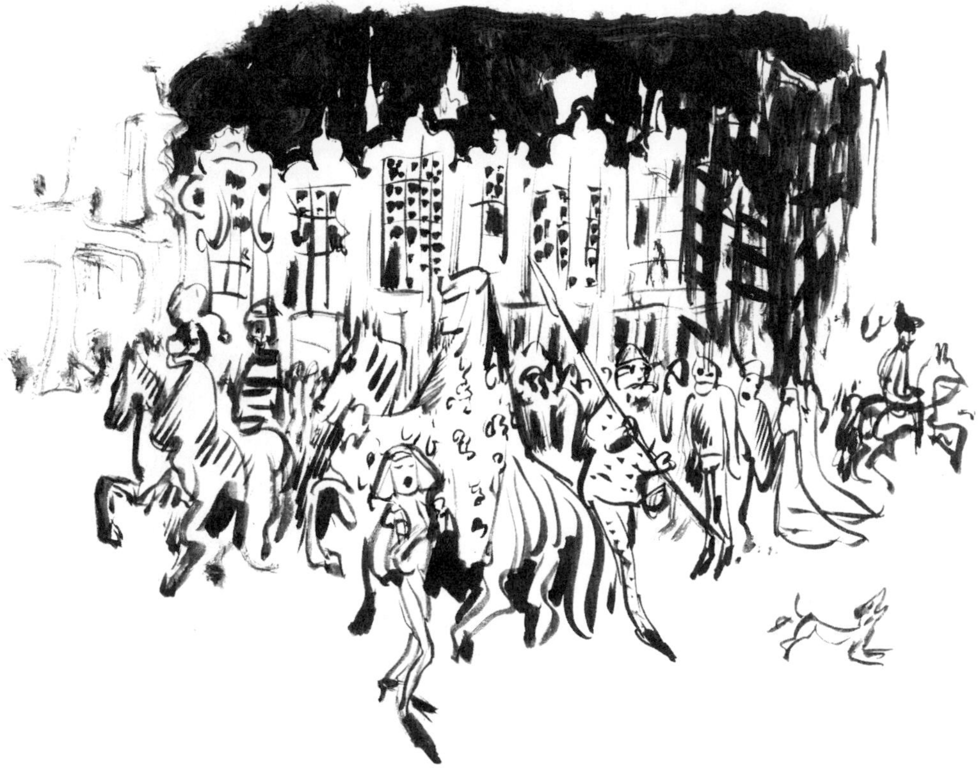

so that amid such
orgies of revelry and ostentation,
even strangers who were comfortably off were
made to feel like beggars.

Of that frantic and colourful life style no testimony remains, save the Maison de Ville, over-restored and over-gilded; the church of Sainte-Gudule, after whom no girl would wish to be named; that sad anachronism, the Manneken-Pis; and a few old streets of gabled houses pompously named after foodstuffs.

Nowadays there are only girls who are almost pretty, almost well dressed; men who are almost smart; fake

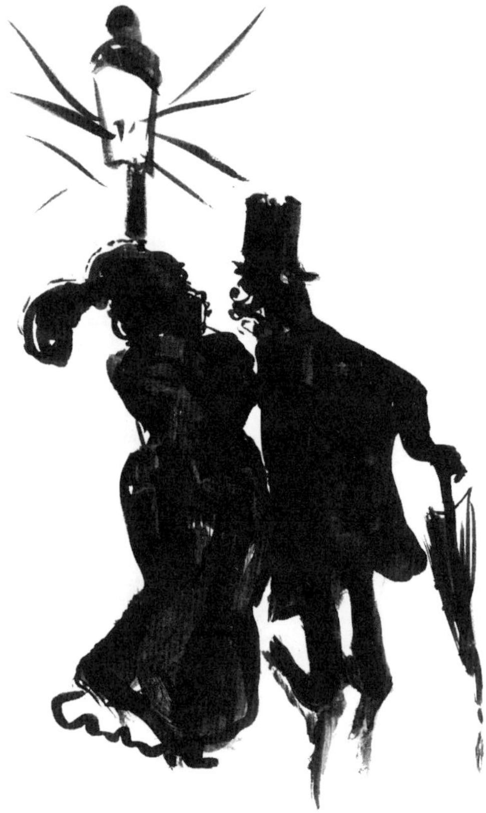

Havana cigars from Antwerp or
Hamburg, and frightful imitation lace made
by machines, although a hundred shops lay claim – as in ancient Greece a hundred cities laid claim to Homer – to the doubtful honour of having supplied the trousseau of Princess Stephanie.

When I went to fetch some luggage from the station, I saw the following inscription over a gate, written (of course) in French and Flemish:

'Way out for passengers without luggage, and for others also.'

That evening, on a street corner, a Flemish woman, quite pretty but stocky, accosted a passer-by and tried to persuade him to go back to her rooms in rue Montagne-de-la-cour, reasoning forcefully that although it sounded a long way away, her wonderful curtains and carpet would make his trip worthwhile.

The King's in on it . . .

We were stopping at the Hotel Bellevue. They had the workmen in. It was being completely redecorated. The corridors were cluttered with planks, ladders and trestles. Thick props held the ceilings up. We waded through plaster and rubble, tripped over pots of paste. The place was supposed to be the last word in modern comfort, or so said the little notices, in English, German, Russian and French, in all the bedrooms.

The waiters would whisper, with a knowing air, and to cheer you up, 'The King's in on it. . . .'

Too true! In Belgium the King's in on everything; only he's never at home. I realised
some days later, when

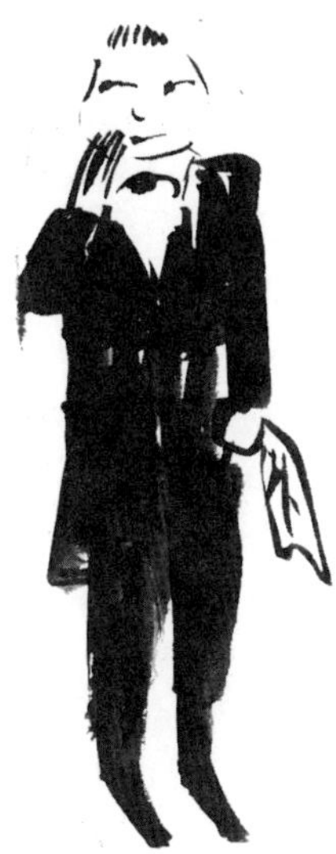

paying the bill, just how deeply the King was involved – too much so. Meanwhile the hotel contained more painters, chimney-sweeps, plumbers, carpenters and upholsterers than guests. Four or five Americans either on their way to Holland, or coming back – they weren't too sure; and a few unfortunate English people who would be off tomorrow to see the battlefield of Waterloo. The service was completely disorganised. There was nothing to be had, not even water. This morning, by way of breakfast, I had a chat with the waiter:

'Monsieur is going on to Ostend, I expect?'

'No, my friend, if you don't mind, I shall go nowhere near Ostend.'

'That's a shame. Monsieur really should go. . . . . It's something to see. Extraordinary thing, sir, since they did away with gambling the Casino has had four tables for roulette and thirty-two for baccarat – all running night and day, sir. . . . And the women, the women! Monsieur is no doubt aware that Ostend is to stay open all year round? Since they did away with gambling, there's nothing to worry about.' Then, discreetly: 'The King's in on it!'

When I said nothing, he continued: 'Oh, he makes no bones about it. Doesn't care twopence for what people think or don't think. He's a right one, he is . . . so long as there's money in it. You should see him arm in arm with Marquet, the Casino director. Now there's a lucky devil. Not so long ago he was just a waiter, an under-waiter, in the station buffet at Namur; many a time he's served me a cup of coffee between trains. He wasn't puffed up in those days – and look at him now, almost a minister. More than that, a buddy of the King's. . . .'

I took my leave.

In the square outside the hotel I noticed a very pretty young woman, neatly dressed in a white summer

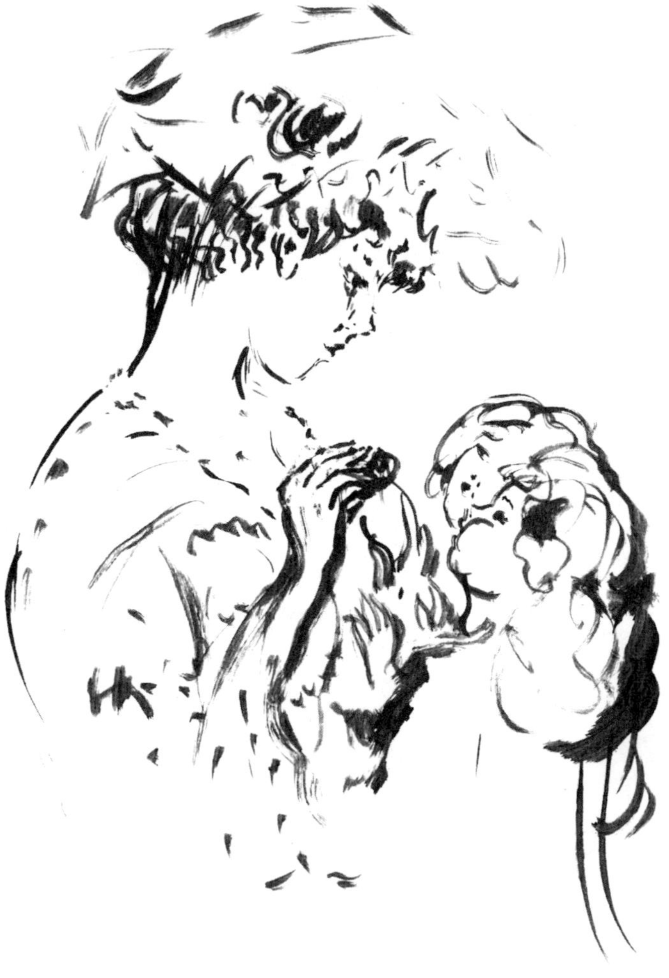

frock, playing with her
two little girls, also in white and
bare-legged. All three were chasing one another around a
tub planted with a large oleander bush. Near by, on a
bench, sat the governess, stiff and severe, a bundle of coats
and umbrellas in her lap, an unopened book in her hand.

Clearly they were awaiting a carriage which, like my breakfast, had not arrived. The hall-porter, resplendent with gold braid, peered anxiously up and down.

The woman looked even more child-like than her daughters. I have never seen such lovely blonde hair, a softer, more graceful neck. Her blue eyes radiated innocence and candour. There was elegance in every movement of her body, every flounce of her skirt. Her arms, her legs, her bosom, her hips were a joyous celebration of life. And although she was slender, even delicate, one sensed that she was rounded and firm, with skin that was suffused with light, like those big white Florence irises at dusk. . . .

All of a sudden she turned and ran away, crying, 'Jeanne, Gabrielle, here comes a big lion!' And when the little girls pretended to scream with fright, she rushed over and swept them up into her arms, smothering them with kisses. . . .

It was evident that she was aware of being the centre of attraction and that she was putting on a show, perhaps for the porter, perhaps for passers-by, maybe even for me: little fluttering gestures, sidelong glances and the like. But I wasn't taken in. I have come across flirts before and know exactly how far they are prepared to go, or rather not to go.

Besides, it would be quite unthinkable for me to have that kind of adventure in a Brussels hotel when nothing of the sort has ever happened to me in any hotel in the world.

All the same, I questioned the waiter.

'She's a lady from Paris,' he explained. 'She stays every now and then. Calls herself Madame X, but we know that's not her real name. . . .'

He bent closer and whispered confidentially, 'Something to do with the King.'

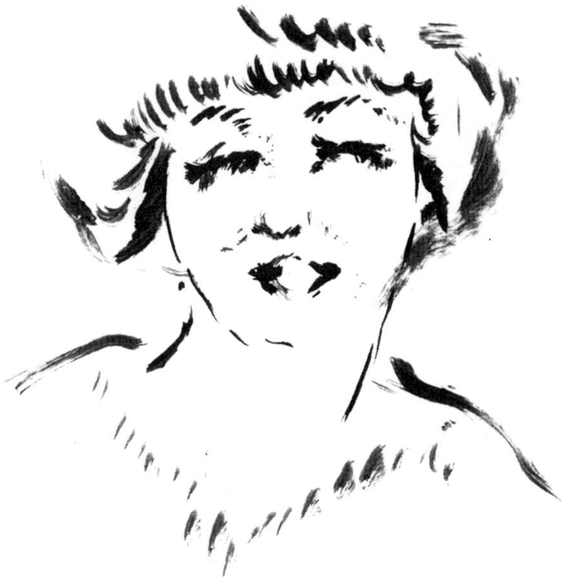

My fellow-spirit

I spent only one good day in Brussels, and that was the day when Mme B passed through on her way from Monte Carlo to Ostend. It is always a pleasure to see her, and particularly to hear her laugh, so I took the opportunity to tell her, quite frankly, what I thought about Brussels, deliberately exaggerating the Belgian characteristics, quite simply to hear her crowing, weeping and choking with laughter.

She has a wonderful gift for making silly people feel proud of themselves by laughing at everything they say, as though she did not know that she looks even prettier when she laughs, because her eyes deepen and glint, like velvet does when you press it with your finger, and her lips, not content with rising to display her pretty teeth, surprisingly reveal her delightful pussy-cat gums. If I were not cured of being in love with love, and capable of becoming enamoured of anything except ugly women, I would envy my friend who is totally infatuated with her, while all she can do is mock him.

Catholicism

The moment you cross into Belgium, you are struck by the prevailing religious miasma, casting a pall of gloom over this little country. Maybe this is why the green foliage is so dark in the countryside which Baudelaire so much detested. Just as in our wild and mournful Brittany, where religion seems to have turned everything to stone, or in the Tyrol, where every bend and crossroads has its holy images which could well be used by the authorities as milestones or road signs, so superstitious religion in Belgium reigns supreme over souls, landscape and laws. Catholicism casts its heavy, unhealthy shadow over the whole country. These symbols of an obstinate faith are everywhere, on roads and footpaths, in the towns, sombre and menacing like those in a primitive Flemish triptych. Centuries have elapsed, progress and science have passed them by, without softening their harsh lines in the slightest.

Some years ago I was suddenly taken ill while staying at a village inn. I asked them to fetch a doctor from the nearby town, which was Ghent.

'Oh, Holy Jesus!' cried the maid, seeing how pale I was. 'Perhaps he's going to die. Say a prayer quickly, sir, say a prayer. I'll be back at once.'

She rushed out without offering any other assistance.

A few minutes later the door opened and the maid ushered in a fat priest, breathless from running. He was determined, come what may, to administer extreme unction. And when I refused to fortify myself with the sacraments of the Church, he protested violently and would not leave until he had called down upon my miserable head all the curses of Heaven and furies of Hell.

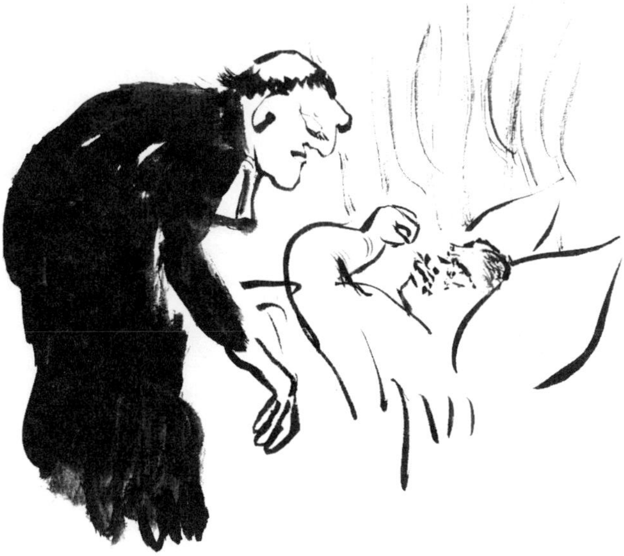

Everywhere you hear the sound of church bells and see processions, extravagant shows of medieval pageantry, packed places of worship, little shrines in bedrooms, bent backs, hands joined in prayer, lecherous thieving priests and terrible bishops with faces like those of the Inquisition. And not even the industrial cities, often a focus of working class discontent, escape this contagion. I once witnessed a strike in Ghent. It was far removed from the popular idea of an uprising – 'floods of humanity battering against the walls like the waves of the sea' – but a religious procession winding silently through the streets, with emblems, banners, standards, women disguised as Blessed Virgins and children as little curly-headed angels. And I shall never forget one ferocious-looking labourer who marched at the head of the throng carrying some object that looked like a censer.

Belgium can never rid herself of the Spanish blood which runs through her veins. . . .

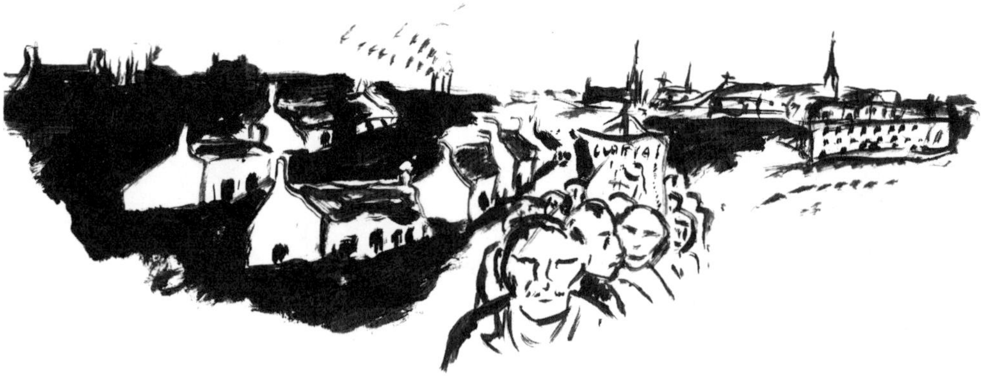

The democrats of Ghent

A charming friend of Maeterlinck, whom we visited in Brussels, told us the story of some strange riots that took place in Ghent a dozen or so years previously. The people were demanding universal suffrage and also sovereign power. They already had a constitutional king but they wanted more . . . a king in ordinary clothes, and one of their own choosing. So they took to the streets, making the usual noises. The middle classes, protected by the troops, looked on indulgently, seeing no harm.

For a while, however, the situation looked dangerous. Shouting, street barricades, revolver shots, musketry, cavalry charges . . . even a few dead bodies. And as skirmishing threatened to continue, the civil guards were called out, our friend being one of them. He himself, and a painter companion, had no option but to side with law and order; the rest were workmen, clerks, shop assistants and the like – almost all in sympathy with the rioters; and they swore, if ordered to open fire on the mob, to aim into the air.

The captain paced up and down looking nervous and worried, ears cocked for the distant sounds of rioting. Occasionally some cavalrymen galloped across the square. The shops put up their shutters, pale citizens hurried home. The noise of the mob drew nearer. Two shots rang out. The captain, a pink-faced man with gentle eyes and a fat, comfortable stomach who kept a haberdasher's shop, turned to the contingent.

'Lads,' he announced, 'it's getting worse. They'll soon be here. I'll have to read the riot act and maybe give the order to fire. But they won't listen. It's awkward . . . firing on your own townsfolk. Deuced awkward. Why couldn't they have kept quieter with their wretched claims? The King's a decent chap, so are the ministers. And they are good chaps, too, dammit! Something could have been worked out. But listen, men! The least possible harm must be done. When I give the order to shoot, only the second rank will open fire. But I wonder if they need to? We only want to scare them . . . three or four dead or wounded . . . maybe that'll be enough to stop the blighters. You there, in the second ranks, attention! Eyes front! I want ten volunteers willing to open fire when I give the command. . . . Five then. . . . All right then, are there four? Oh, come on, speak up!'

And astonishingly, from one end of the line to the other, came the word. Me! Me! Me!

Out of the fifty men in the ranks, only two remained silent . . . the painter and my friend.

Fortunately they aimed very badly. Only ten poor devils killed and twelve wounded.

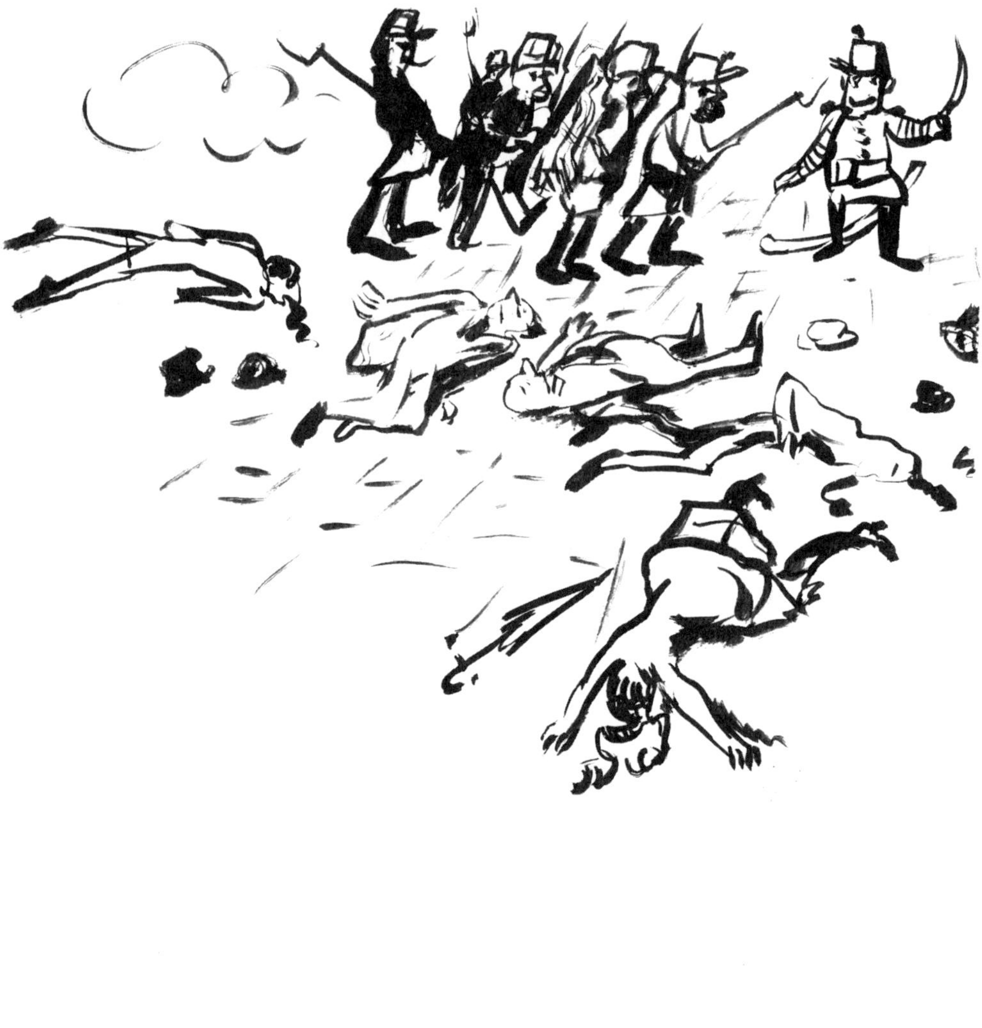

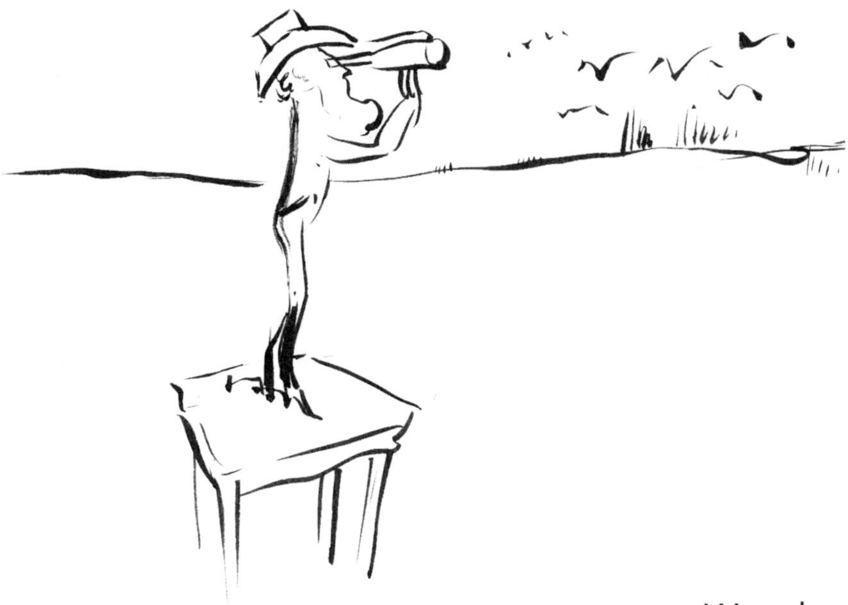

Waterloo

I decided to have a look at the battlefield of Waterloo. Perhaps I was subconsciously driven to make this absurd visit by the equally absurd notion that I ought to accustom myself to the idea of defeat, loss of nationhood, Belgification, which is what the name Waterloo conjures up for me.

But I saw nothing on the battlefield of Waterloo. Near the inn of the Belle Alliance, where a few English tourists were swopping little yellow pebbles for little black pebbles, all I saw, standing upon a table, booted, Panama hat askew and holding an enormous telescope to his eye, was M. Henri Houssaye, peering out at . . . what?

Some crows were flying to and fro over the melancholy plain, and I thought to myself sadly – he must still take them for eagles.

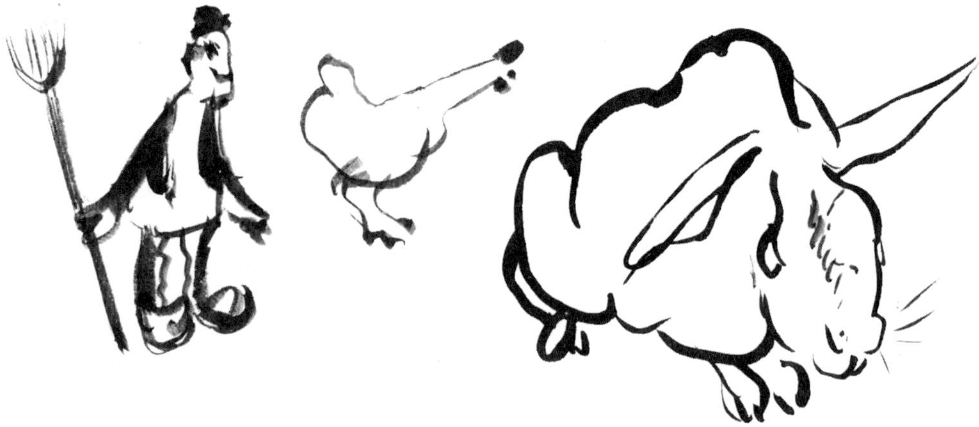

Selective breeding

The Belgians are great breeders of chickens, and also of rabbits. They have produced one kind of rabbit which goes by the grandiose name of The Flemish Giant; and for a rabbit, hardly an animal to inspire poetry, he really and truly is a giant. The Flemish Giant can yield as much as twenty-two pounds of meat.

But the most important and flourishing industry is poultry-farming. I visited one farm near Brussels, owned by M. de S. A good enough fellow, who was soon telling jokes and jovially digging me in the ribs. His laugh was so loud that I instinctively covered my ears, as when a whistling locomotive passes. His farm was marvellous – food, care, hygiene, physical exercise, selection – everything aimed at the well-being and improvement of the poultry. I have never seen such care lavished on human beings.

'I'm strict,' confessed M. de S., 'but I never upset

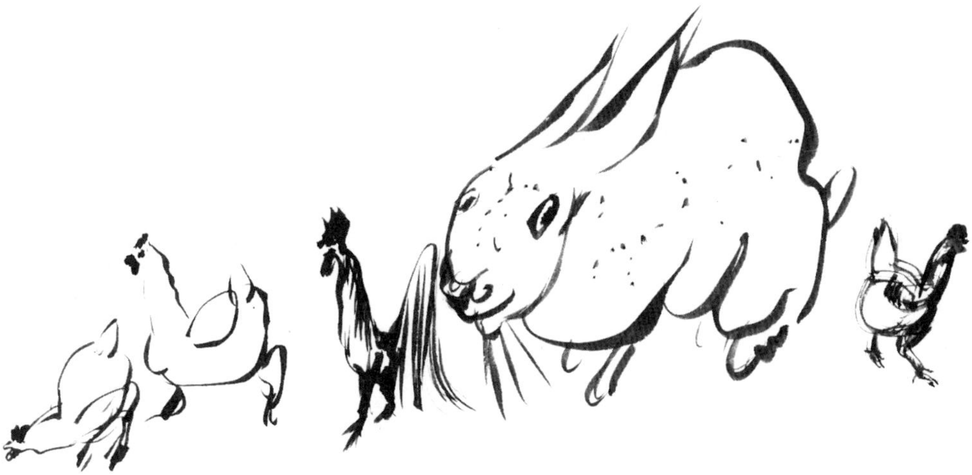

them. You must always keep them happy. If they're unhappy, they waste away. Then it's goodbye to your eggs!'

When I remarked on how lively, strong and contented his birds looked, he agreed. 'Ah, that's it! One has to be ruthless and scientific. I eliminate the cocks that don't crow clearly and loudly. It's all in the crowing, my dear sir. The louder a rooster crows, the more passionate he is, more eager to breed. A fine voice in roosters, as in men, is always a sign of . . . well, you know. . . .'

'So tenors,' I ventured. 'I had never thought . . . .'

'No, not tenors, of course. Nothing but softies, wets. Only fit for the spit! No, I only keep the baritones, proper well-endowed baritones. The hens know it. The more the cock baritones, the better they'll be served, the more they'll lay . . . bigger eggs, stronger chicks. Listen, I've founded a club in Brussels to spread these biological truths all over the world. A colossal success, my dear sir. We have magazines, lectures, laboratories – heaps of money

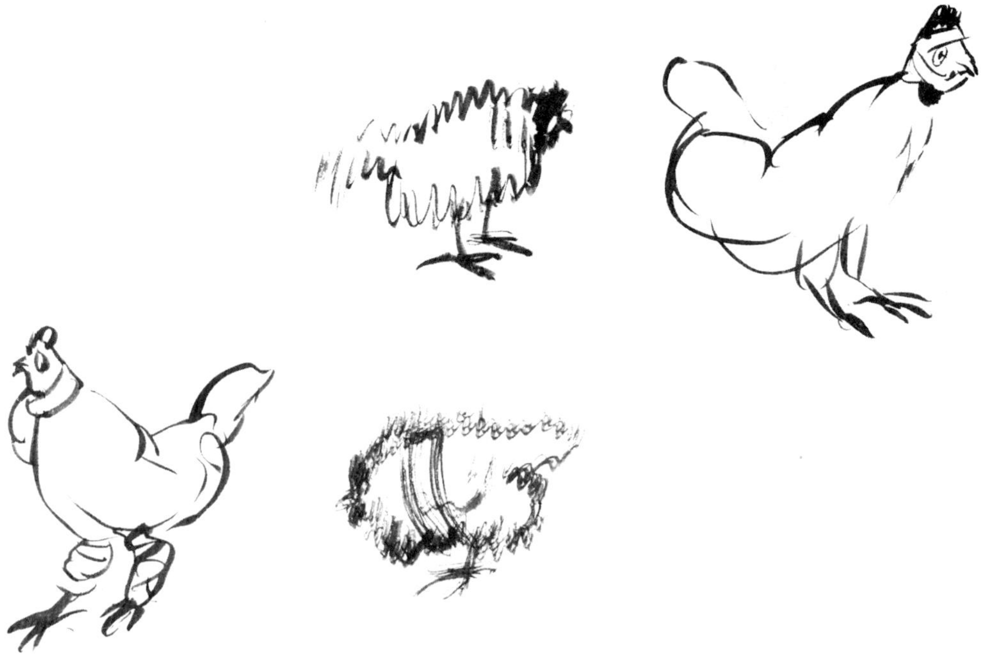

– exhibitions, song contests. It's a regular academy of . . . well, you know. Fascinating.'

He informed me that the only way to restore a declining breed was through incest. 'You take, say, a couple of wild birds with all sorts of unacceptable defects – criminal things with grey, black or white plumage, spindly legs, tails too long, with traces of earlier cross-breeding. You isolate them, their eggs hatch, you pick out a cock and a hen, brother and sister . . . and so on from clutch to clutch. After five or six generations, you get back all the proper features, all the original purity of the race. Oh, it's absolutely fascinating.'

He reflected. 'With human beings, by Jove! I wonder . . . .' and he gave me a nudge. 'Hey, what do you think? The breed's been going downhill in France. Might try it there, eh?'

Royal gossip

I was dining with friends from the foreign colony when the talk switched to the King. I learned little that was new. For example, the King is intelligent, sly, devious, unscrupulous, passionate and quite devoid of pity. He is grasping and greedy, and a megalomaniac into the bargain, which impels him to build, build, build – houses, palaces, shops, simply in order to make Brussels a grand city on a par with New York or Chicago – quite idiotic, because he is dealing with Belgians and not Americans. To satisfy his pleasures and his greed, he is obsessed with amassing money, even by the shadiest means. His business acumen is extraordinary, inexhaustible. He swindles people – and countries – and has turned his throne into a well-organised business, a kind of broker's office where he deals in just about anything, including scandal. His heart is proof against all feelings of justice and goodness. Beneath the veneer of elegance, charm and perfect manners he conceals a core of pitiless ferocity.

One of my friends, a civil servant, admitted nonetheless that he was fond of the fellow and gave an instance of his quick thinking and humour. 'At one time,' he said, 'every shop window was full of picture postcards of the King and Mlle Cléo de Mérode in all sorts of compromising positions. These used to upset him a lot – not so much because they were treasonable but because they were crude and stupid. Although he banned their display, with heavy penalties, their sale continued "under the counter".

'You have heard, no doubt, of your fellow countryman M. B?' my friend asked.

'The King's double?'

'Yes.'

'Certainly . . . same height, same build, equally well dressed, same square beard, same eyes . . . uncanny!'

'Right. Well, one day last year the King was strolling along the front at Ostend with some friends. He mixes so freely with the crowd that people hardly notice. As he passed me I was standing in front of a kiosk which was liberally decorated with those same cards. Imagine my amazement when the King turned back, left his friends and came over to the kiosk.

' "Good morning, my dear M. C," he said to me affably. "Very pleased to see you, what? Hear you won some money last night – a great deal of money. . . ."

' "Yes indeed, Sire, it's true enough. I was very lucky."

' "Splendid, splendid. . . . One has to make money, my dear chap, lots and lots of money."

'He bought a paper and put it into his overcoat pocket. Then he glanced up at the display of cards, the least improper of which showed him with Mlle Cléo sitting practically naked on his knee, pulling his beard. I was a bit worried, though somewhat amused, as you can imagine.

'Having concluded his inspection, he pointed to all that filth in the most natural way and remarked, "Would you believe it? Poor old B! After all, he must find this muck rather upsetting. I know he comes quite often to Ostend these days. So get all this cleared away quietly, will you?" And, after shaking my hand, he rejoined his friends.'

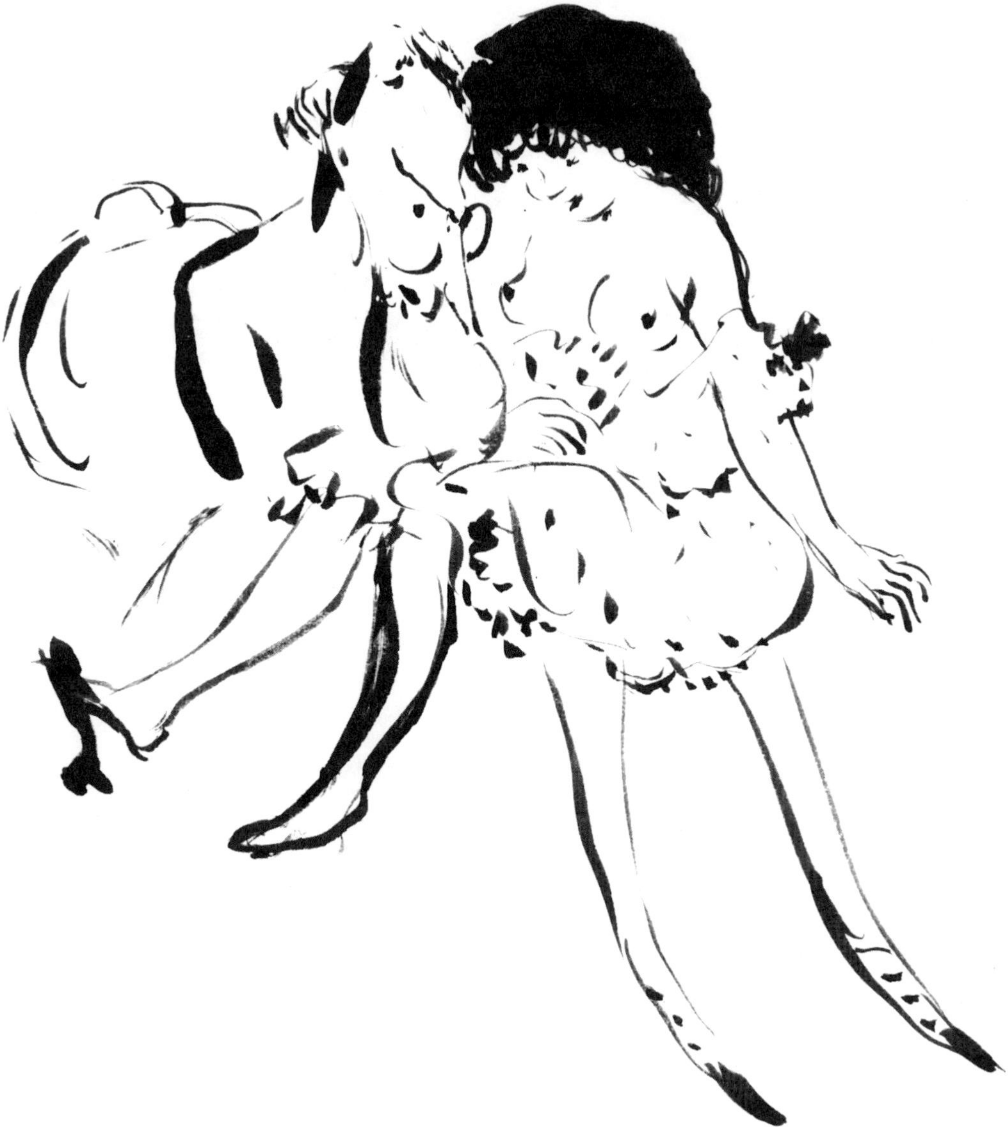

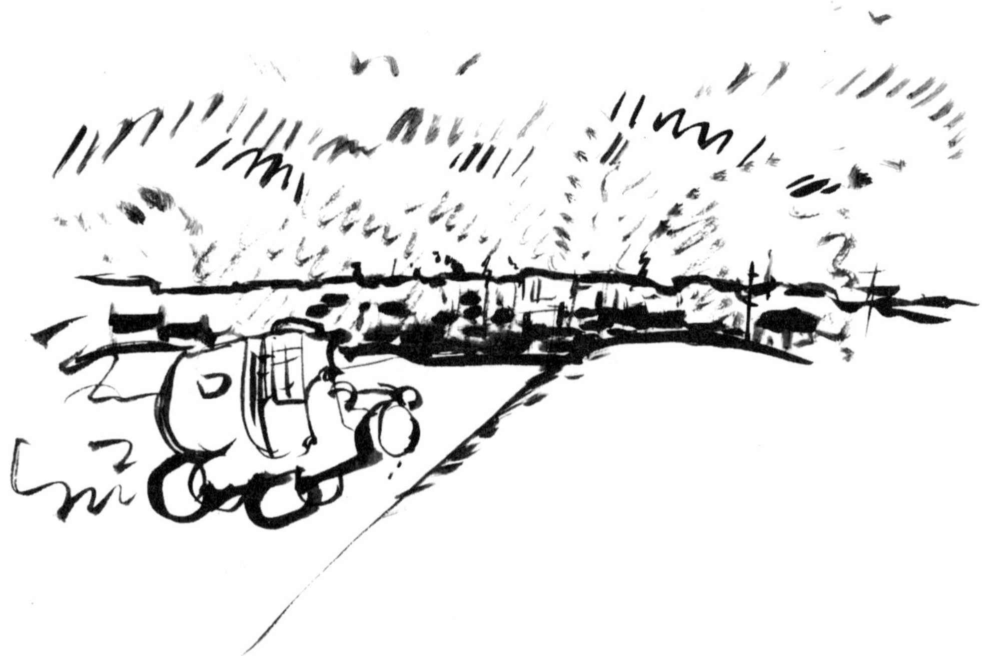

On to Antwerp

We set out for Antwerp, so glad to leave Brussels that even at the risk of breaking our springs and splitting the crank-case on the inevitable cobbles, we averaged 55 kilometres an hour and reached our destination in three-quarters of an hour. The good old CGV stood up to the strain miraculously and not a bolt came loose on the way. At times she hardly seemed to be touching the ground. She flew, she sailed

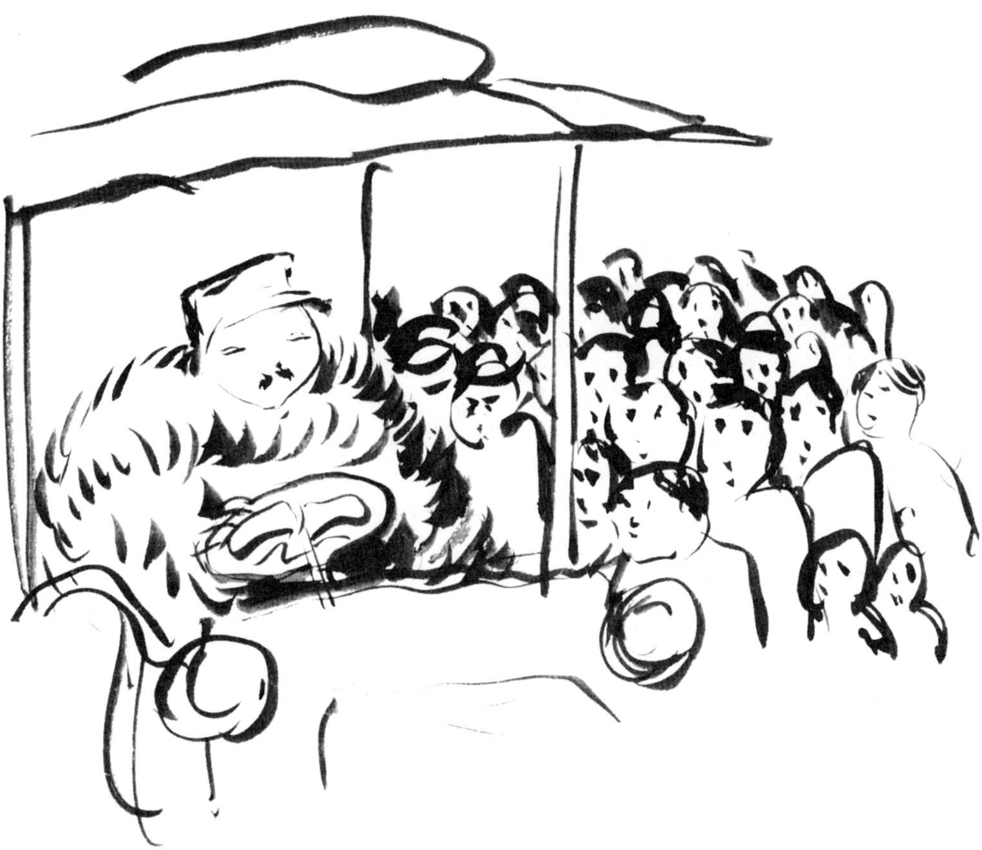

through the air like a balloon . . . and suddenly there we were.

Whether cars are a rare sight in Antwerp I do not know, but certainly ours caused a sensation, almost a riot. The moment we stopped outside a restaurant, a crowd gathered, small boys at first, then women, but keeping a tidy distance as if it were about to roar off or charge. Gradually they came closer, summoning up the courage to touch the chassis, the gear-lever, the handbrake, the clutch, even to undo the bonnet catches and after a few minutes a growing mass of people surrounded the car. Brossette had his work cut out. I was afraid that he might let some tactless word or gesture escape him and then where would we be? You never know with crowds, they are as impressionable and foolish as women. Brossette, too, was an object of curiosity. Because of the cold wind he had put on his wolfskin coat, and this astonished them greatly. Some laughed and poked fun, others seemed scared to see a human being dressed as an animal. One wit asked him whether he ate cows and sheep alive, and why he didn't go on all-fours like a dog, instead of sitting up to beg like a man . . . .

I was a bit concerned about getting the car safely through the crowd, which was getting larger and noisier, but the restaurant owner smilingly reassured me. 'Don't worry', he said. 'They're only having fun. After all, they don't see big motor cars that often.' Then, scratching his head, he observed, 'Just the same it might be sensible for your chauffeur to take off that . . . well, yes, his skin. It's that skin of his . . . .'

He went outside, flapped his napkin, said something to the crowd and approached Brossette. Then, to our amusement, he reached out very cautiously and touched the skin.

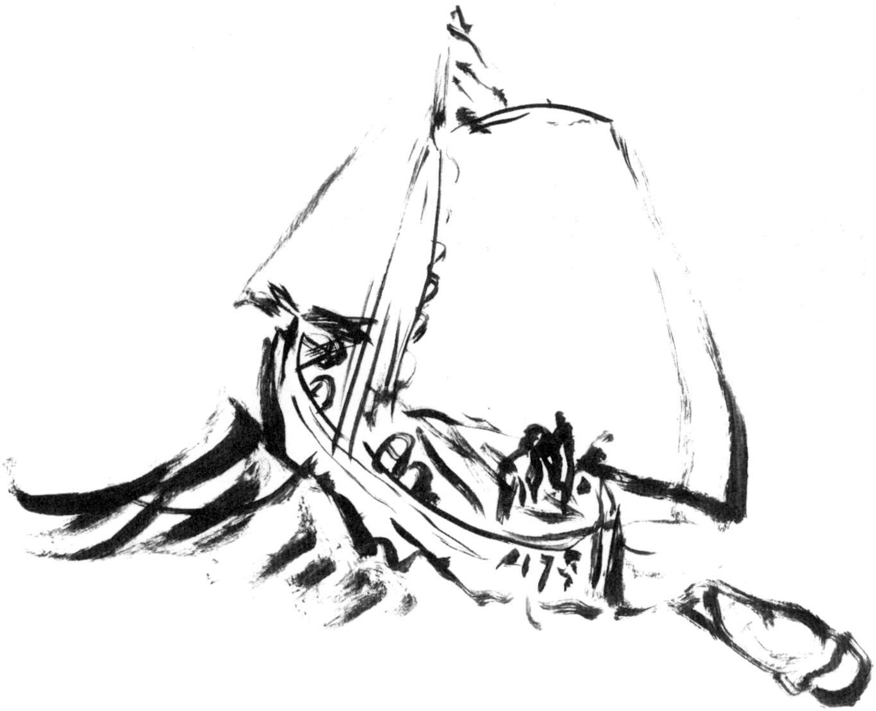

The docks

I love harbours, just as I love boats –
all of them. A boat is one of man's boldest inventions and by far the most elegant. I often ponder, affectionately, on that unknown individual who one day sat down beside a pond, watched a pretty little red-headed teal come floating by, and promptly invented the boat. Of all the machines which man's sensitivity and imagination have created to rid him of a thousand servitudes and bring him closer to nature, I prefer the sailing boat and the motor car.

Less frivolous and varied, less colourful than Marseille, the port of Antwerp is hardly less imposing –

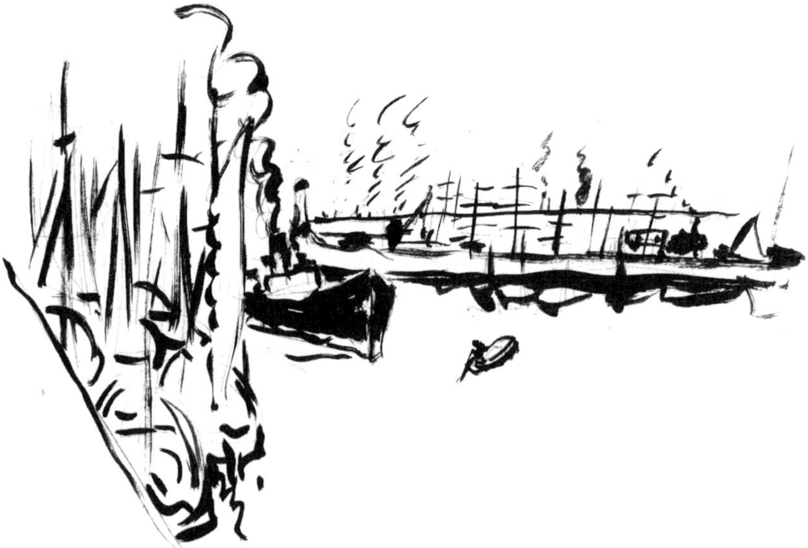

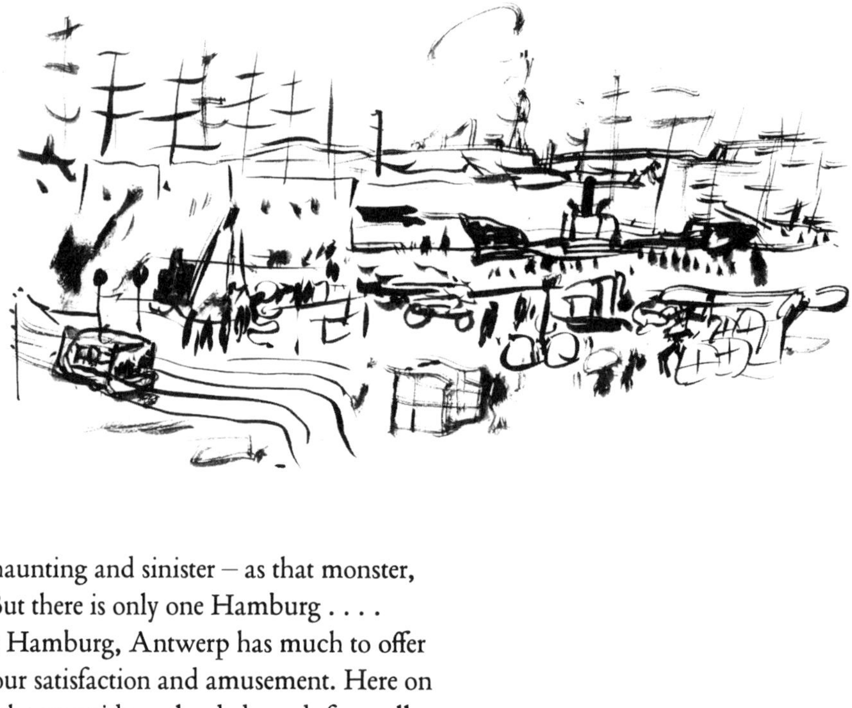

although not as haunting and sinister – as that monster,
Hamburg. But there is only one Hamburg . . . .
Yet after Hamburg, Antwerp has much to offer
for our satisfaction and amusement. Here on
the quayside are landed goods from all over

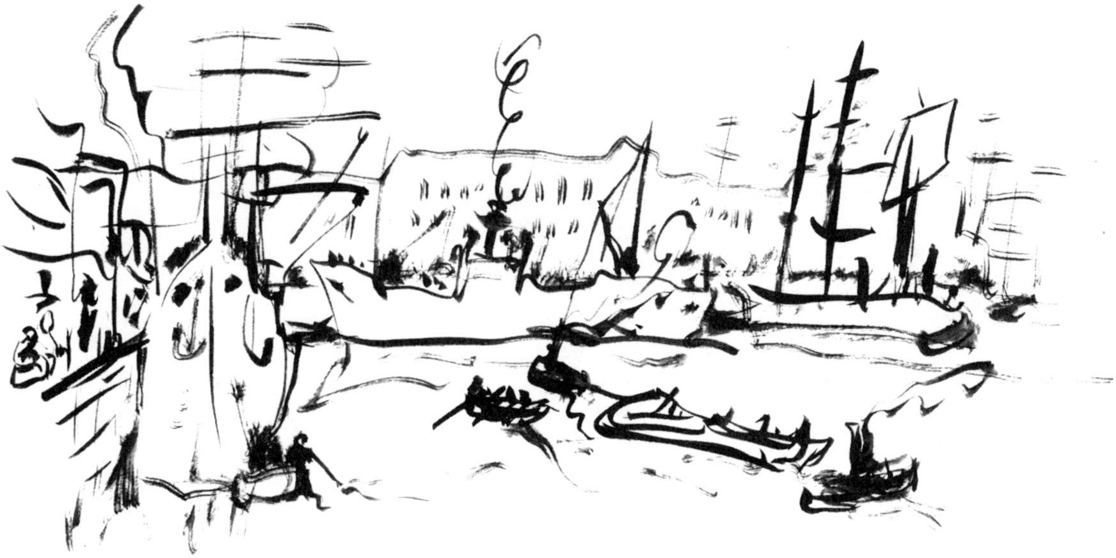

the world. Side by side, the railway and canal systems provide a constant interchange of commodities: bales of wool for metal, ivory for clothing, machinery and toys; fruit, rare plants and spices, oil, rubber and exotic timber for printed cottons, perfumes and the coloured beads dear to the African's heart. Liners with gleaming fresh paint stand gaily out to sea, while returning tramp-steamers, blistered and barnacled, limp into port for a much-needed refit. From the same quayside crews also set forth, sailing into the unknown to make their fortune. Some of them will never came back; while others will return, unrecognised and recognising nothing and nobody, unknown even to themselves . . . strangers.

A great port is a marvellous and novel sight – an astonishing world which contains the entire universe . . . .

Minstrels

A couple of negroes, dressed in tails and dented toppers, red scarves around their necks, were entertaining a crowd of idlers, workmen, cabin-boys and clerks. One danced, the other sang. His song went like this:

In my country we got forests,
In them forests they got trees,
In them trees are plenty branches,
In them branches plenty birds,
And in all them birds is music sweet,
Some little flute, that goes 'tweet, tweet . . . .

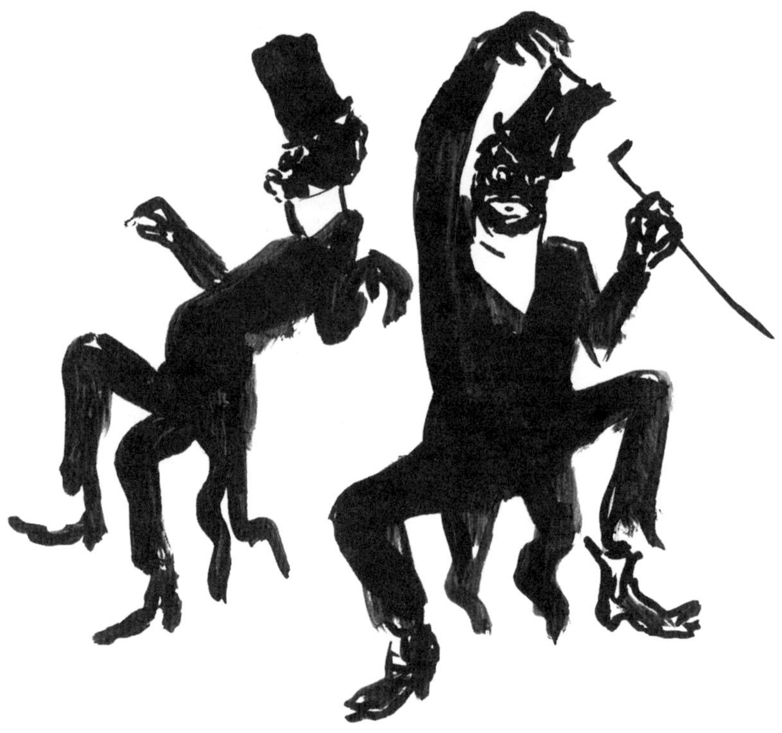

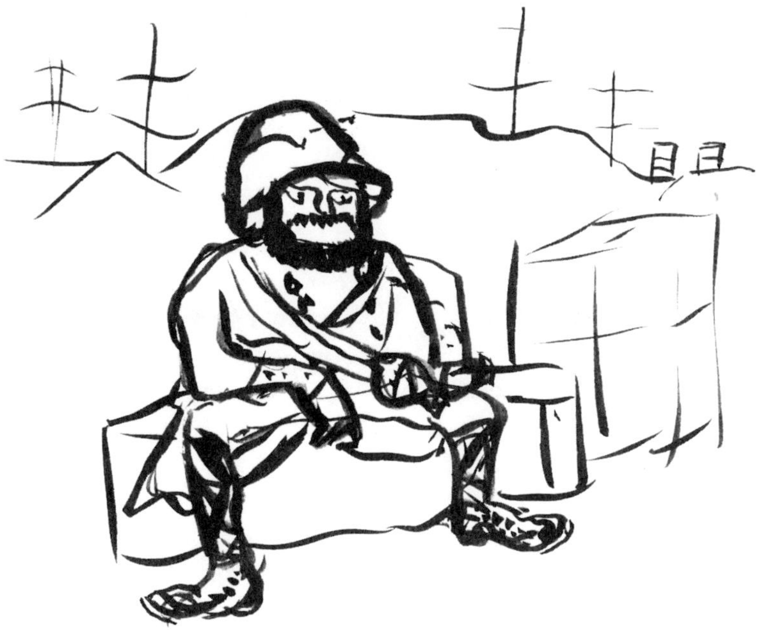

The missionary

The man sitting on his luggage beside the gangway was, they said, a compatriot of mine, a missionary. A bearded figure in boots and an ill-fitting sun-hat, his greasy cassock tucked up like a soldier's greatcoat, he was exploring the mechanism of a Browning automatic. The pistol was strapped to his belt beside a big-beaded rosary. Sun-tanned and forceful, by the look of him, but with gentle, smiling eyes. A decent chap, for sure, but more like a bandit than an apostle. I found this reassuring and went up to speak to him. He was off to Fiji, he explained, with a cargo of gramophones.

'You'd never believe,' he said, 'how ignorant and pig-headed those black blighters are! It's odd, but I just can't convert them. I've tried everything, but it's like knocking your head against a brick wall. Nothing does any good: God the Father, Virgin Mary, Saint Joseph, the joys of Heaven . . . they don't give a damn, you've no idea. I've known some blackies in my time, believe me, but nothing like this lot. Listen: booze or no booze, it's all the same, can you imagine? I mean, alcohol is bloody marvellous for conversion. God knows, they get tight as ticks, but that's as far as it goes. Just as heathen afterwards as before. It's unheard of . . . probably unique. But this time, I've got them. I'm trying this gramophone stunt. What have I got to lose? From what I've heard, the gramophone works miracles. A friend out in Africa has had marvellous success – and all quite painless: no worry, no strain, no catechising. He sits the blackies down around the instrument, and after three records . . . presto! they're Christians. Grace descends on them as they listen.' He chuckled. 'It's not really surprising. Natives love music and singing. We'll see now whether I get on better with brass bands, Strauss waltzes, Yvette Guilbert and Caruso than with God the Father, promises of Paradise and tots of rum. In any case . . . .'

He let out a hearty laugh. 'In any case, my journey won't have been wasted. I give you my word that if I don't manage to convert them – and even if I do – they're going to pay me for those gramophones, and give me a damned good price too. I can't lose. I'm taking out a thousand with me, thanks to a wealthy old lady. A marvellous woman, indeed, a real saint on earth!'

He put his pistol back in its holster and gave his rosary a twirl, with a great clatter of beads, crosses, sacred hearts and holy medals.

'It's a good thing', he concluded, 'that from time to time we come across devout and noble souls like her, because religion nowadays, you know, is becoming a swine of a job! Still, there we are . . . .'

Pogroms

Workers from Hungary and Roumania, Serbian peasants, groups of Russian singers are setting sail for America. Their indifference is painful to see. Handsome women in filthy red garments and cheap brass jewellery drag along their children, crying with hunger, tiredness and bewilderment, like so many bundles. What will become of them and will their exile ever end? They are driven down brutally into the steerage, cooped up like cargo – which is what they are – in the depths of the hold for days and nights beyond counting, thrown together higgledy-piggledy, in the stench of their filth and misery, without air or light, and virtually without food, under the harshest discipline . . . .

The most pitiful emigrants of all are the Jews, from many lands, seeking some corner on earth which cannot offer them hospitality but which may free them, if ever so slightly, from the contempt of their fellow men, and help them break the chains of their terrible burden of infamy. I followed a group of them, dressed in rags, yet gesticulating eagerly and showing an intelligent interest in everything, an enthusiasm for life which one seldom sees on the faces of other people. How cruel and stupid it is to destroy so much valuable energy, inventiveness and progress by massacring them in barbarous countries like Russia, or boycotting them in civilised countries such as France.

My attention was drawn particularly to an old man, with a very long beard, seated a little apart on a sack of old clothes. Like most of his companions, he wore a frock-coat that had once been black, and a peaked cloth hat. His face was blank, with more distress etched on it than if he had been weeping, all the fatigue of suffering

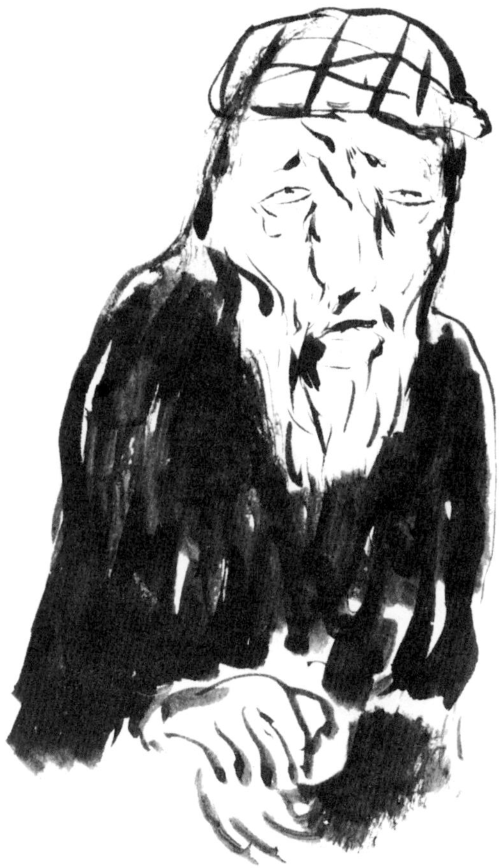

humanity. Yet the eyes in this ravaged face were youthful and gentle. I reproached myself for intruding but could not bring myself to leave him.

When he noticed me, he smiled and murmured, 'Bonjour, mossié!' I held out my hand. He trembled. His soft hand lingered awkwardly in mine for a few moments and at first I did not catch what he was saying. I listened, as one listens to the sound of the wind or the sea, to that melodious voice with its rolling rs and sing-song end syllables. He was comparing himself with Job, and kept repeating, 'Yobb! Yobb!'

I sat on a wooden chest nearby and he told me his sad story.

As a young lawyer, he had been forced to leave his poor village in Russia after a dispute with an anti-Semitic magistrate, and settled in Paris with his wife and three children. There he made a meagre living selling, among other things, sugared almonds. His partner had robbed him and his landlord had flung them out on the street. A Jewish charity helped him to return to Russia and he opened a small outfitter's shop in a little southern town. He lived there with his wife, six children and brother-in-law, a rabbi, for sixteen years. He planned for two of his sons to become lawyers, one to be a doctor and the two youngest to study engineering. The daughter did embroidery.

One evening, during the early days of the Revolution, a troop of soldiers swept down their street and fired through the shop windows. His youngest son, hit by a bullet, died in his arms and he himself lost consciousness. When he came to, the shop was in darkness and the sound of firing came from every direction. By the light of a candle he saw that not a garment was left on the shelves; everything had been looted. At the back of the shop, amid a bloodstained heap of broken drawers, lay the body of his wife. She had been strangled.

He described all this in a matter of fact way, without obvious anger, and it was my own eyes that filled with tears.

'They took the bodies . . . buried them that night, shovelling them all in, dead and wounded together, no one knows where. The massacre of the Jews and the looting continued for several days. We couldn't resist, Mossié, how

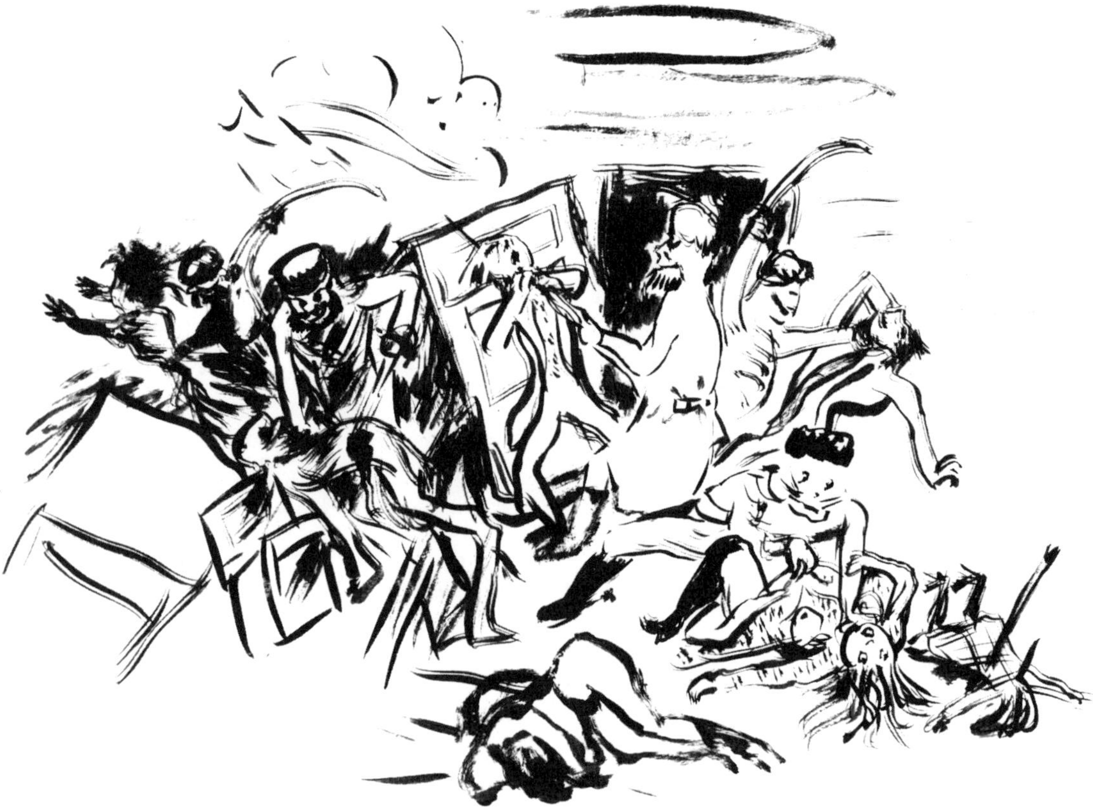

could we? They beat us, kicked us, spat on us . . . .'

Fires were left to burn and most of the Jewish quarter was destroyed. Of the family of nine, only five got out alive. After wandering from town to town – often being driven out with stones – he found a job in a bank. Two of the boys worked as railway porters, his daughter sold oranges. As he was working on the accounts one evening with his sons, there were sounds of firing and once again soldiers burst in, shooting and howling like savages. The old man was wounded in the neck with a bayonet. He removed his scarf and showed me the scar. 'Why am I not dead? Those dragoons and gendarmes are worse than wild beasts. They get drunk, attack the women, attack the children . . . slashing and killing – and always laughing!'

Later in hospital, he learned that his sons had been shot, his daughter killed and mutilated beside her barrow of vegetables and fruit.

And so the terrible saga continued. He fled once more with his grand-daughter, surviving another Cossack raid on the restaurant of a hotel where he had found temporary work, and eventually being rounded up with others accused of harbouring anti-government terrorists. An officer ordered them to raise their hands, but the child, not understanding, stood smiling at him. Her grandfather's cry of warning came too late. The officer shot her down.

'She didn't utter a cry . . . just some blood on the cobbles . . . like a little bird. A tiny thing.'

The old man's beard twitched, he wrinkled his nose, but he did not weep. The source of tears had dried up forever. He was silent for a moment, then shook his head. 'Why am I going? I don't know . . . . Stupidity, stupidity!'

And I found myself incapable of saying anything at all.

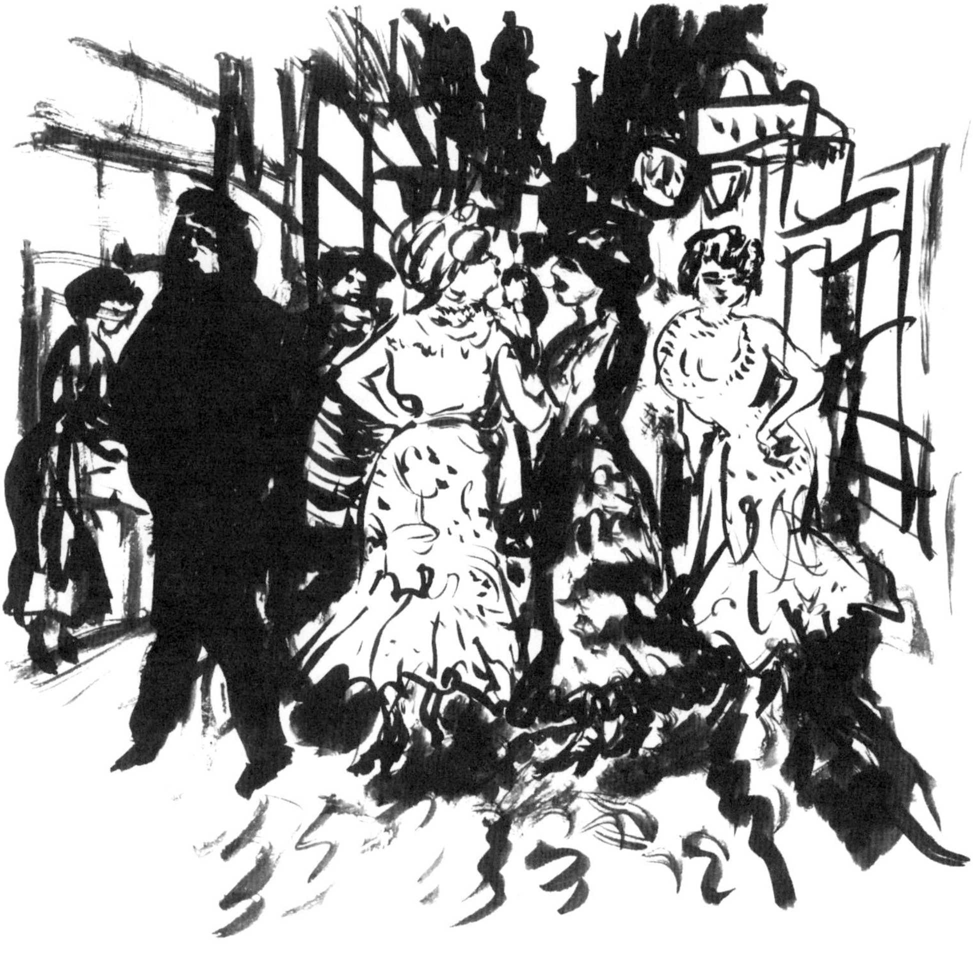

Prostitution

As I strolled along the quays, now so broad and spacious, my mind went back to the Antwerp of thirty years ago, to the narrow, twisting alleyways where prostitutes, in pink slips and spangled petticoats, openly touted for custom on

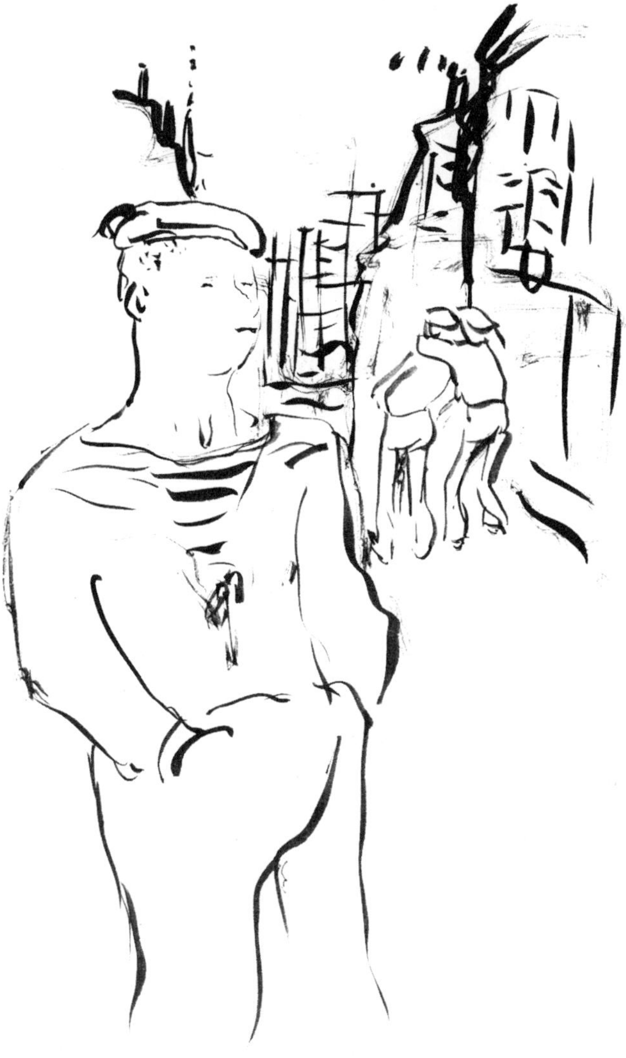

the dockside, as at Le Havre, Marseille and Toulon.
Gross, drink-sodden women, plastered with make-up, paper flowers in their hair, sat waiting for clients or dozed, heads resting on bare arms. I remembered how difficult it was to fight one's way through to the docks, past

those dark, airless, stinking hovels, the rubbish, misery and filth. Gone by that time were the oriental splendours of the Rideck, where families could wander in safety. Like mass and vespers, the Rideck was part of a ritual, a pleasant Sunday afternoon out. There were picturesque little shops and cafés, marvellous sounds and scents, and everything nicely cleaned up for visitors.

I only knew the Rideck from hearsay. My recollections, sadly, were of debauchery in the streets, of shouting and screaming, of sailors lurching after the tarts, yelling like overgrown children. And I recall
from those days a black girl from
Kotonu in Dahomey –
tall, slim

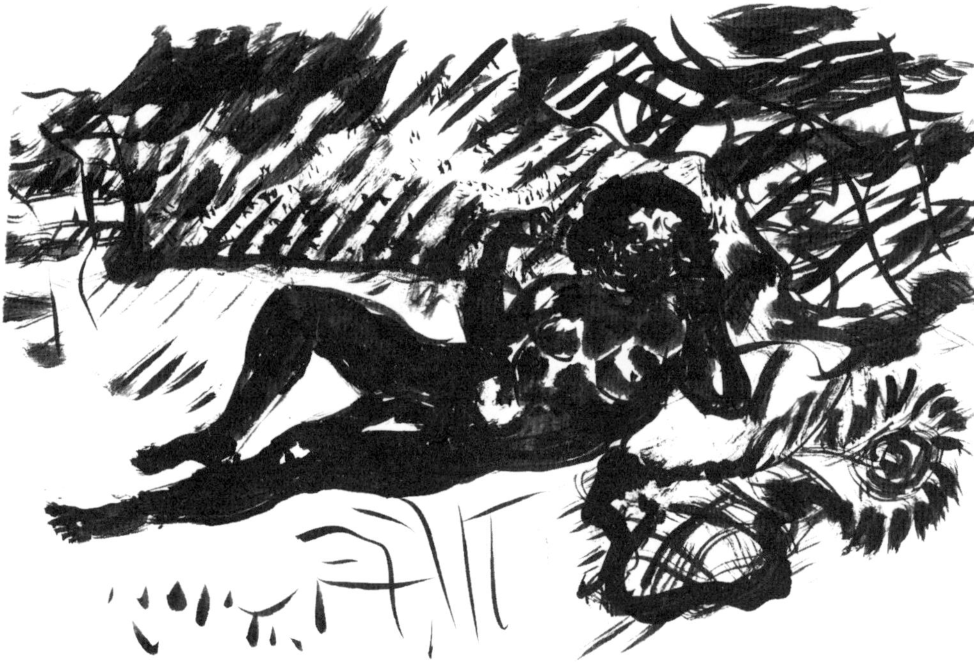

and willowy, naked on a yellow silk mattress, reeking of perfume, brass bangles on her arms, and a purple dahlia in her hair. Her deep black skin had a golden sheen and her smile was dazzlingly white. She could speak a little French, for she had worked for a family in Bordeaux and then in a Paris brothel before being brought here to Antwerp, a cold, grey place which she hated. On one stiflingly hot summer's night she prattled away, in a rather incoherent manner, about her homeland, which she only dimly remembered.

'The palace of our great king at Kotonu is unbelievably beautiful', she said. 'All your buildings are just miserable shacks. It has great thick walls, all pink, and hardly any windows. You enter through a low door guarded by fearsome tattooed warriors. The roof is flat and completely covered – or tiled – with severed heads. Very fiddly work – it takes clever artists to fit those heads together, like mosaic. But the king is himself an artist, and he wants it all beautifully and neatly done, so that the rain cannot get through. The effect in the evening, as the sun goes down, is lovely and the smell delicious . . . . But that sort of roof is not very strong. The heads fall apart, or the vultures get at a few, cracks appear and rain starts dripping into the palace. Then our great king dispatches his witch-doctors through the land. Wearing terrible red-horned masks and brandishing huge cutlasses, they yell, "The royal roof needs repairing . . . ." And soon the palace is looking splendid, as good as new!'

She seemed rather sad, her thoughts far away. Doubtless she was walking around the moats which surrounded the fine city of Kotonu. The jackals were howling, and she was breathing in the delicious, nostalgic scents blowing from the charnel house . . . .

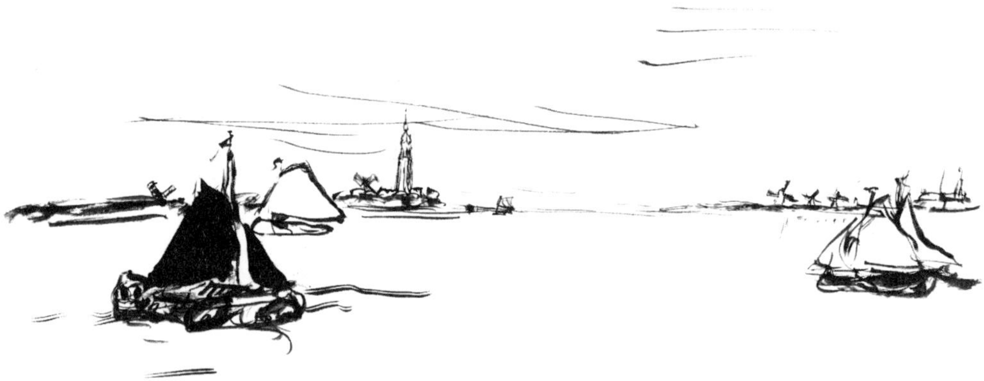

Motoring in Holland

As we headed for Holland, I found my heartbeat quickening and my eyes peering eagerly ahead for a first glimpse of that longed-for horizon. I don't mind admitting I was feeling very moved. By a stroke of irony, however, I had been on Dutch soil for a good ten kilometres without being aware of it. We might have driven all the way to Dordrecht without realising it had not a helpful peasant put us right. So we turned round and made our way back to the border to make our peace with the customs . . . .

Holland proper – the Holland of water and sky, the infinitely pearl-grey Holland – begins on the other side of Breda. Roads become smooth, springy and dust-free, surfaced with well-laid bricks. The dyke roads are planted with huge trees – elms, planes and *blancs de Hollande*, the roots of which plunge deep into soil as rich in humus as in moisture. Flocks of starlings and lapwings skim the water that is everywhere, glinting below the cover of vegetation like coals glowing in a brazier beneath a layer of ash.

You have to drive slowly across the polders, along the dykes. They are very narrow, usually bordered by canals and intersected by little humpbacked bridges and drawbridges that you don't notice until you are on top of them. Whenever you meet a horse, one of those fine animals with a noble neck and withers, you have to stop and assist the carter or rider, for the horse is the same stupid creature everywhere, and here the danger is all the greater because of his size and the limited space available.

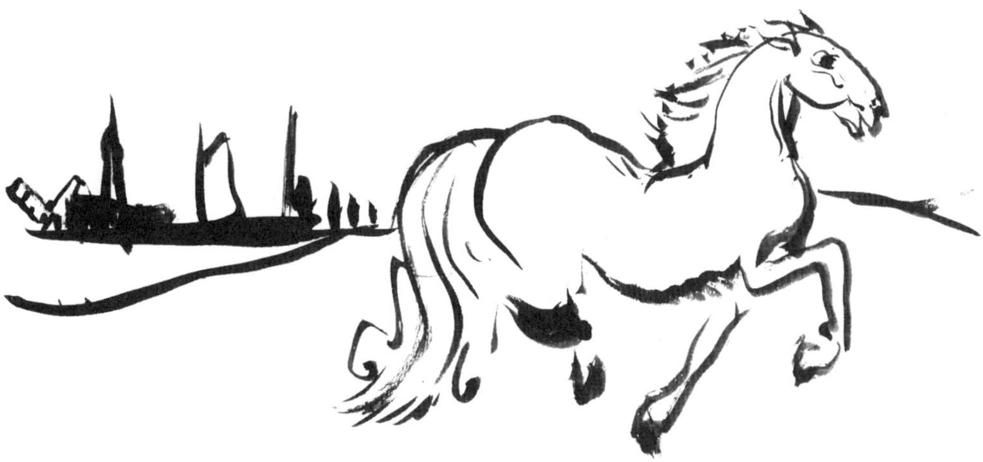

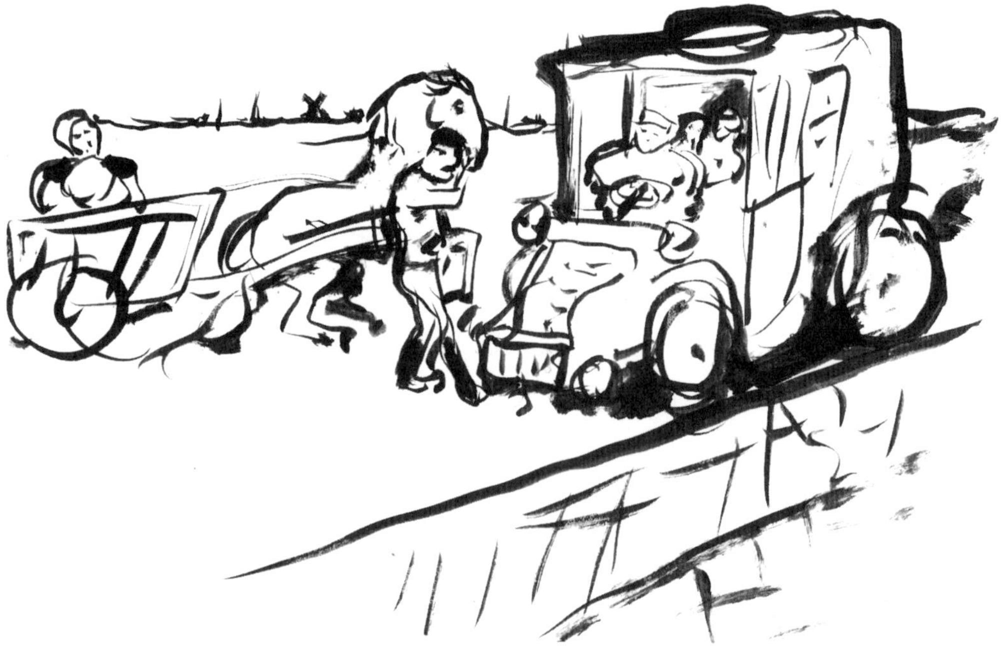

Otherwise there is no rule of the road for cars except those you make up for your own safety as you go. You can even tumble into the canal if you feel so inclined – provided you and your machine are fished out at your own expense. The slightest skid or momentary inattention on the part of the driver may do the trick, for at any instant the road is liable to end in a sheer drop at the water's edge.

This kind of motoring, with its continual interruptions, is at first irritating. Brossette never stops grumbling, 'Rotten country', but even he soon gets used to it, as we all do. Indeed it makes a pleasant break. You get to know the people, see how they live and, in a way, share their life.

Vincent Van Gogh and Breda

Breda is the town where Vincent Van Gogh was born, and where he lived for some time when he was young . . . . I was astonished not to find any affinity between the artist and his birthplace. I would like to have obtained some information about this phase of Van Gogh's life, or failing this, to see his house, and perhaps the first scenes that he saw and stirred his feelings. But when I asked anyone, people merely gaped at me:

'What's that you say? . . . . Vincent Van Gogh? . . . A painter, you say? . . . Haven't you got the name wrong? . . . In Breda? . . . . Don't you mean Amsterdam? . . . Hang on a minute.'

Nobody knew him.

I explained that he was a great, pain-ridden artist who died, still young, in France, not all that long ago. That he was famous in France, Germany, even Holland . . . and that there were paintings of his in the museum at Rotterdam . . .

'It's possible,' someone admitted. 'Van Gogh, eh? No, doesn't mean anything to me. There are a lot of painters and a lot of museums in Holland!'

I tried to remind them of his tragic face, his stubborn forehead, his frenzied gaze, his short fair beard.

'Fair beard, eh? Plenty of those around here . . .'

'But listen,' I blurted foolishly. 'Don't you remember? He was so good with children, he spoke to them . . . .'

But they weren't listening to me. They sidled away, casting me suspicious glances.

Poor Vincent! He wouldn't have minded being ignored by his compatriots. He wasn't looking for glory, but for something even more impossible: the absolute. And he died of it . . . .

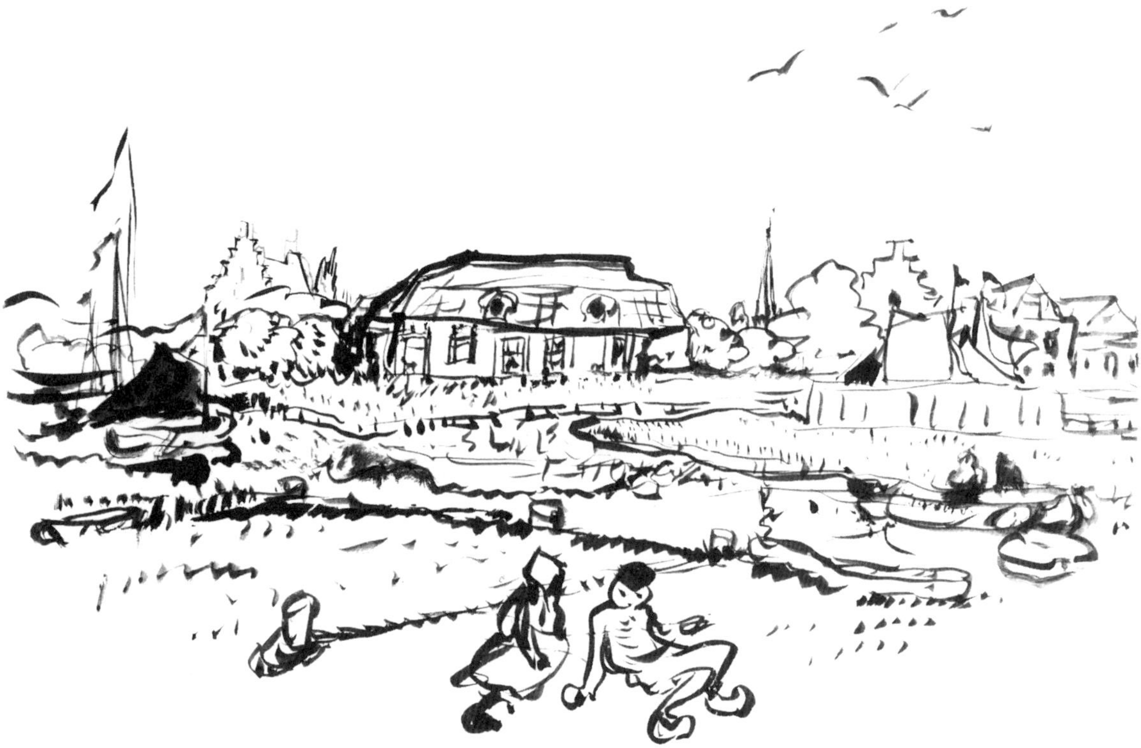

Gorinchem

The little town of Gorinchem – the name is a combination of Rhine and Meuse – and virtually unknown to tourists, is a sheer delight. I was enchanted with the place, like a child with a new toy. For although it is very old, it is beautifully clean. The streets are so narrow that as you drive past you can almost touch the fronts of the brightly painted and varnished houses. The streets, too, are washed clean, like the flagstones in an interior by Pieter de Hoogh, and paved, so it seems, with the same mosaics as those used for facing the houses. And the shop windows, with their exotic fruit, rich fabrics and lace, and heavy silver jewellery, are gleaming . . . .

We stopped at a cake shop to have tea and watched the people passing by. Their faces were much alike, good natured and rather dull, the sort you see in old prints of tulip growers. They would gaze at the car, unsure as to whether they should admire or disapprove. Then they looked at one another and wandered off without saying a word, to be replaced immediately by another little group. Some of the women were blonde, others very dark, with oriental complexions. Fishermen pushed little carts piled with nets and baskets of salmon. In a doorway a child was selling picture postcards of quaint churches, windmills and barges on canals. Life flowed by, today as every day, a constant stream of people, their clogs making a gentle clatter on the stones. . . .

Claude Monet's discovery

I was entranced by the little bridges straddling the waterways, the symmetry of the single wooden span and its reflection; little round bridges, like those in Japanese prints . . . and the low wrought-iron gates that open on to front gardens with flower beds that gleam especially brightly in this damp country where light suffuses and caresses the landscape.

I realised for the first time that most Dutch towns and villages have a distinctly oriental flavour. They evoke the art of Japan, of China and of the Indies and all the enchantment of lands bathed by oceans and of distant islands, as if the Dutch seamen who visited them had brought back, along with their rich merchandise, affectionate memories of how they looked.

During our tour I recollected the day, some fifty years previously, when Claude Monet, who had come to Holland to paint, unwrapped a package and saw for the first time a Japanese colour print. He was so excited and overwhelmed at the sight of that astonishing technique, in which so much life and movement was contained in a single line, that he could only gasp, 'Almighty God!'

It was at Zaandam that this miracle had occurred: Zaandam with its canal, ships at the quayside unloading timber from Norway, fishing smacks moored side by side, its narrow creeks, pink shanties and green houses – the most Japanese of all Dutch towns.

In a nondescript little grocery store a fat man had been wrapping customers' purchases – a pennyworth of pepper, sixpennyworth of coffee – in sheets of paper

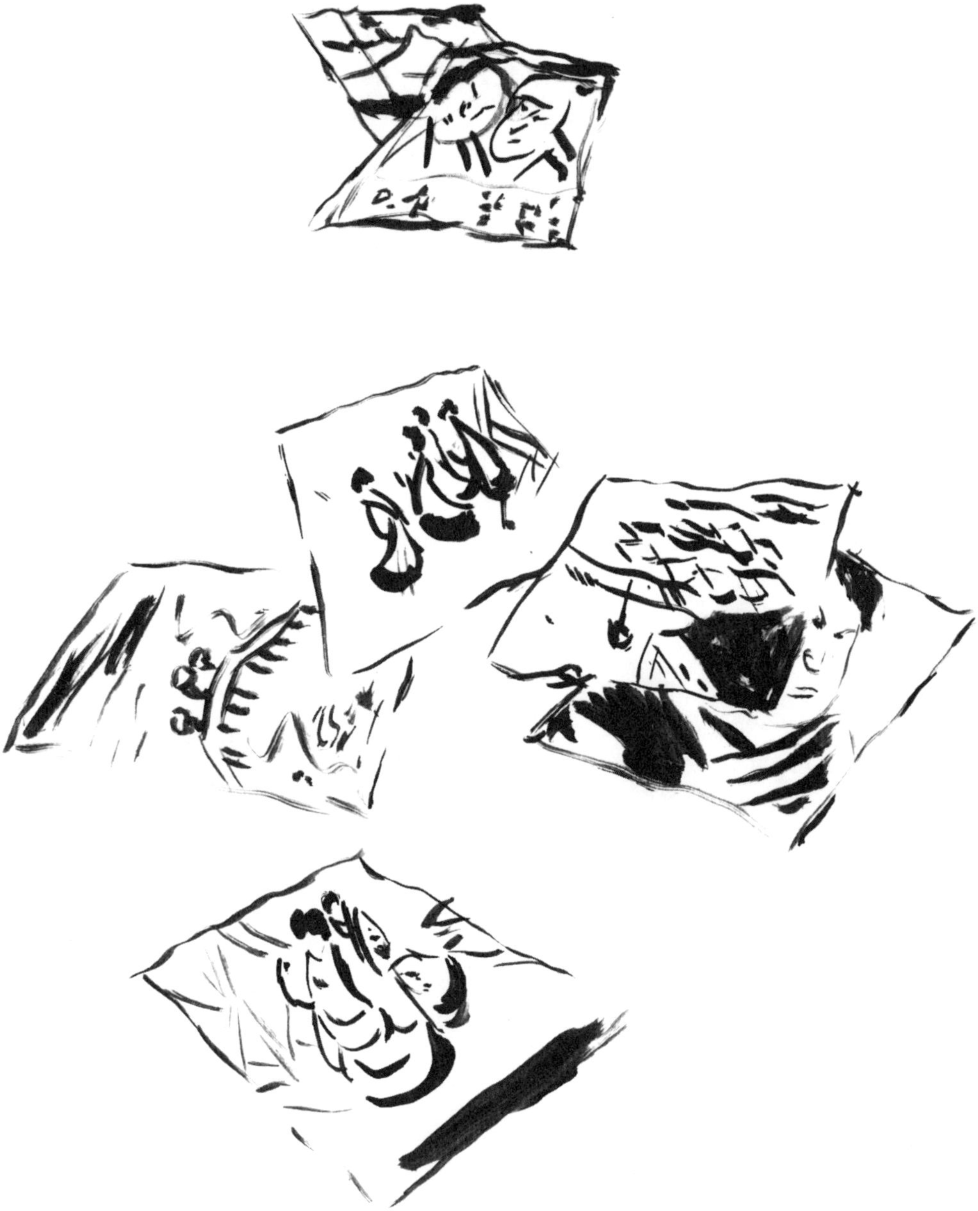

brought back, together with the spices, in some ship's hold from the Far East. They were, in fact, glorious drawings by masters such as Hokusai, Utamaro and Hiroshige. Although not wealthy in those days, Monet resolved to buy the shop's entire stock. There was a pile on the counter. His heart leapt. The grocer was serving an old woman, and reached out a hand. 'No! No!' cried Monet. 'I'll buy that. I'll buy all you've got!'

With the air of someone humouring a child, the grocer handed the whole lot to Monet. 'Take them', he grinned. 'You might as well have them. They're not much good – not strong enough. My own paper's best.' And he wrapped the old woman's piece of cheese in a sheet of brown paper.

Back at his lodgings Monet spread out his pictures. Some of the finest and rarest – though he could not know that – were by Hokusai and Utamaro: women at their toilet, women bathing, seascapes, birds, trees in blossom. One particularly breathtaking example showed a herd of does; he learned later it was by Korin.

An amusing anecdote but one of real historical significance. For it laid the foundations of a famous collection, and represented a turning point in late nineteenth-century French art.

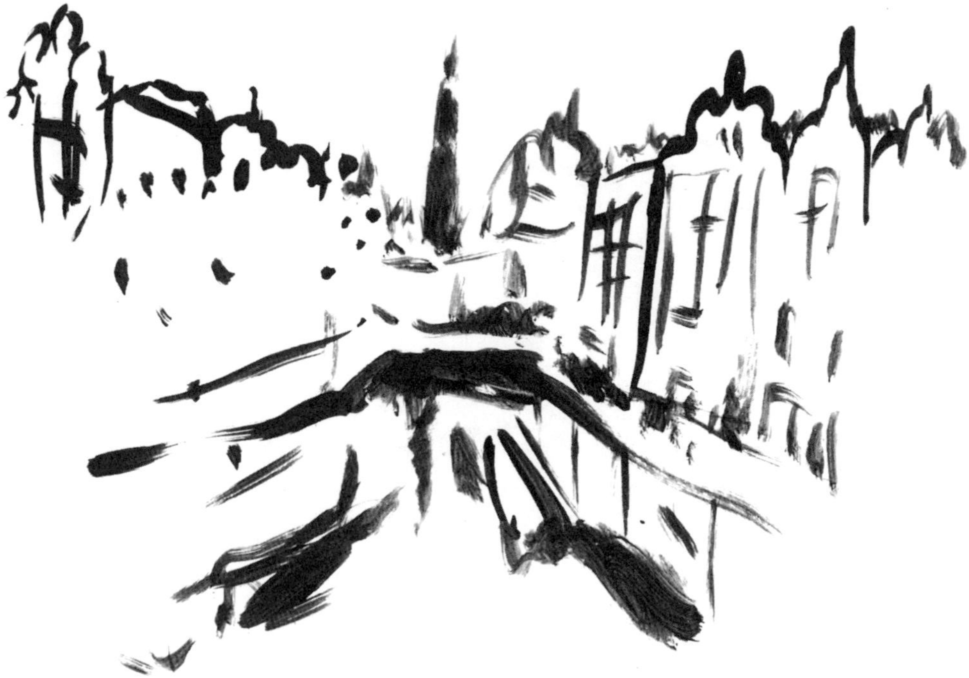

The canals of Amsterdam

If one does not know them well, and if one lacks an acute eye for details and differences, all the Amsterdam canals tend to look alike. One of my friends declares that it is all 'frightfully monotonous'.

But I have visited Amsterdam often enough to understand that nowhere is more diverse, more changing, than Amsterdam; no two reflections of the houses in these similar canals are alike, and furthermore no single house is like another. Every stretch of canal reveals a different landscape of walls, gables, barges, window-boxes; every house has a face of its own, and its individual structure according to the extent to which the supporting piles have subsided. And above it all is another prodigious landscape of sky . . . .

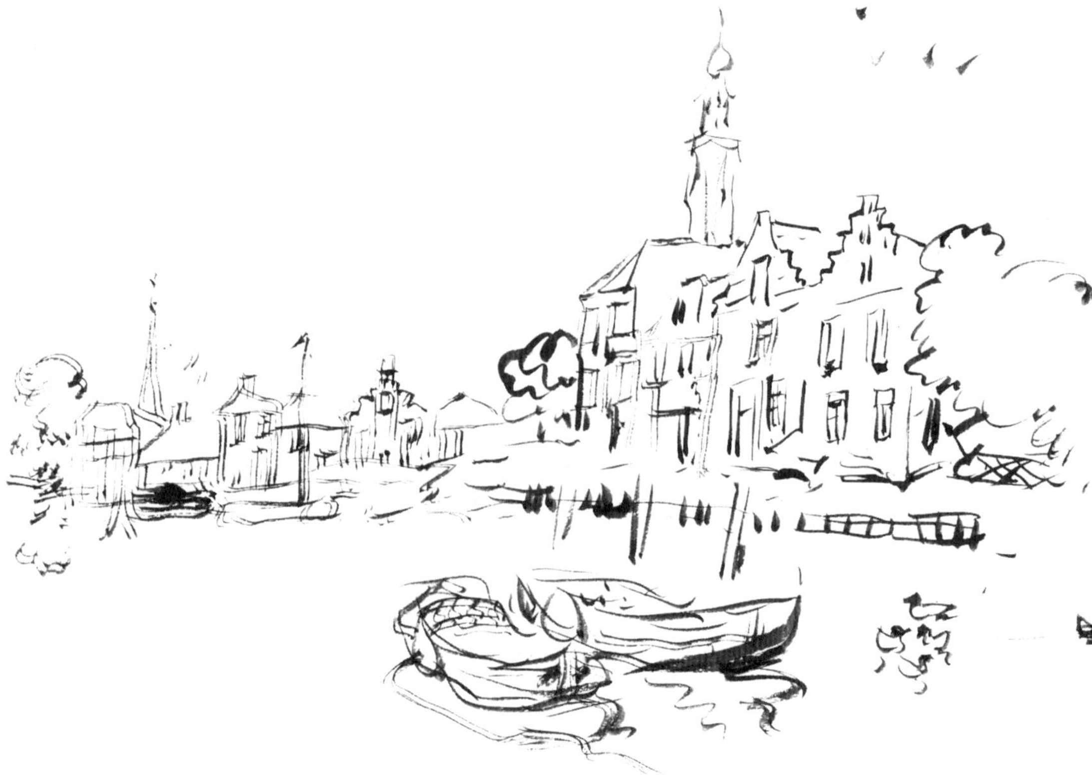

Rembrandt

Rembrandt's name is inseparable from
that of Amsterdam, where he lived for so many
 years and where he developed his great gifts to the full . . . .

Amsterdam, whose inhabitants dress in black like those of Venice and show a similar taste for loud voices and heavy jewellery. In both cities the sun works the same magic with sky and water. Surely it would not have been the same had Rembrandt been born in some sleepy inland town and never seen the sun gilding the docks and the dark waters, casting its effects of light and shade on ships' hulls, making the very air glow. Perhaps what he drew from his inner self would have been sufficient to astonish mankind. But I rejoice to discover in his works not only a feeling for forms but also for sumptuous colours, born of the interaction between his genius and the teeming life of a great harbour, of Amsterdam in particular, most oriental of all western ports, Amsterdam and its sombre population of Jews.

Closing my eyes against the intolerable glare of the setting sun into which we were driving, I reflected on the artist's sad end, the last years of misery and misfortune, expiating perhaps the crime of having dared, for our benefit, to steal the divine fire of heaven's light.

Evening in Dordrecht

The sun was already clipping the horizon when we found ourselves at Dordrecht, which, after we had passed through so many tiny villages, seemed huge, partly because of the time of day, when everything is magnified. The Meuse – or rather the Merwede – was as busy as a city street. The ferry was not there and we had to wait an hour before we could cross . . . .

As we were finishing our meal a party of English people sat down at a corner table next to us, the men in dinner jackets, the women in evening dress. One very young lady with fair hair was constantly jumping up and wandering around. Even when seated she was always fidgeting with something – her fan, a gold-tipped cigarette, her rings or her hair. Under the chair she was continually kicking off her shoes and putting them on again – pretty little silver slippers and white silk stockings. When some remark made the men roar with laughter and caused the ladies to lower their eyes, the fidgety little thing blushed to the roots of her hair. My eye caught hers, and in it I read her anxiety as a desperate toe failed to retrieve an errant slipper which rolled beyond reach. She blushed even more deeply, so that I even imagined the white stocking turning pink, before the questing foot finally disappeared into the elusive slipper.

That night I slept soundly,
without a dream . . . .

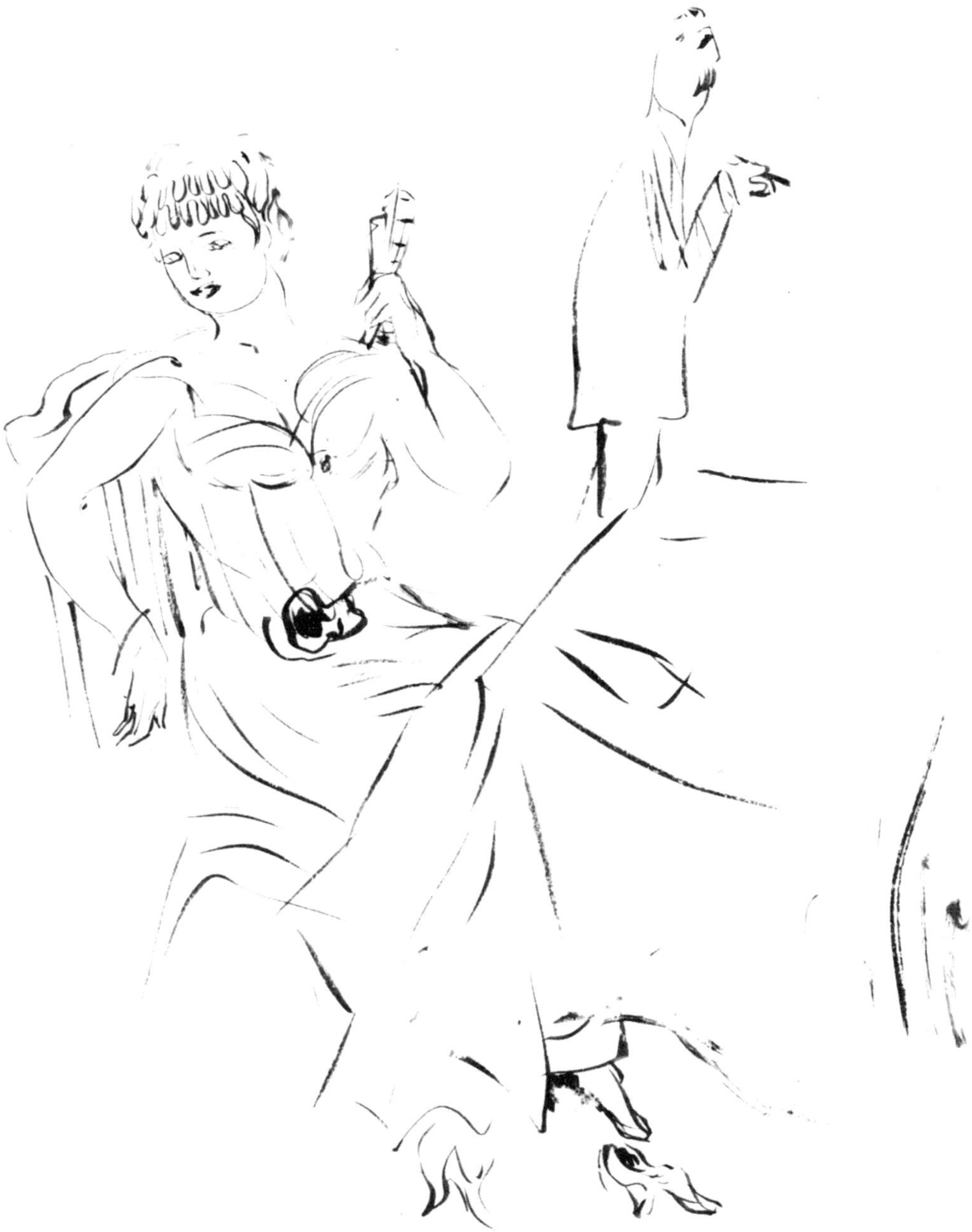

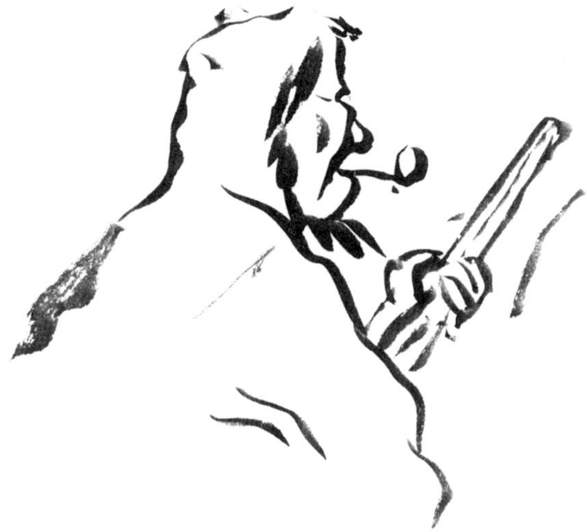

The Boer museum

The only museum we visited in Dordrecht moved me so much that we went to no other: it was the Museum of the Boers. They, no less than the Master of the Death of Mary, Pourbus, the Breughels, Jan Steen, van Ostade, Cuyp and van Goyen, are truly of Holland and the Dutch School. Despite the climate, the weather and the soil, and the need to adapt to new ways of life, they have retained the same hard, placid expression, the same sturdy build as their urban counterparts, but allied with something of the cowboy's loose, springy gait.

This handful of Dutch farmers took with them to the tip of Africa all the virtues that have made their Dutch compatriots at home rich; composure, tenacity and daring. But as Puritans, they have applied them to living upright, harsh and primitive lives. They have hardly mixed their blood with those of other races, and they have disdained the fortune-hunters and adventurers who are always attracted to partially unexplored countries. . . . Is it that the

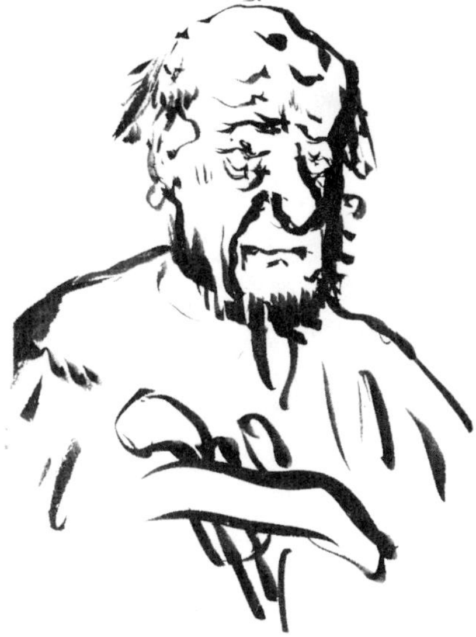

virtuous pastors, who went out to share a life of agriculture and religious austerity, were unaware, as they tilled and prayed, of the riches lying at their feet? Did they despise them or were they simply unable to exploit them? In any event they were forgotten. . . .

The attendant of the museum was in the garden, an apron round his waist, a rabbitskin cap on his head, lifting some hyacinths. With a disconsolate air he showed us a wooden table with piles of dusty postcards and illustrated catalogues that nobody ever bought. When the museum opened he had been given, by way of local colour, an enormous Boer hat, a sort of khaki tunic and some leather gaiters.

'And I had a cartridge-belt across my chest.' He sighed. 'Now I haven't even got a cap with gold braid on it like my colleagues. . . . And do you know, President Kruger was in Dordrecht one day and didn't even come to the museum. President Kruger. Exactly! Ah well!'

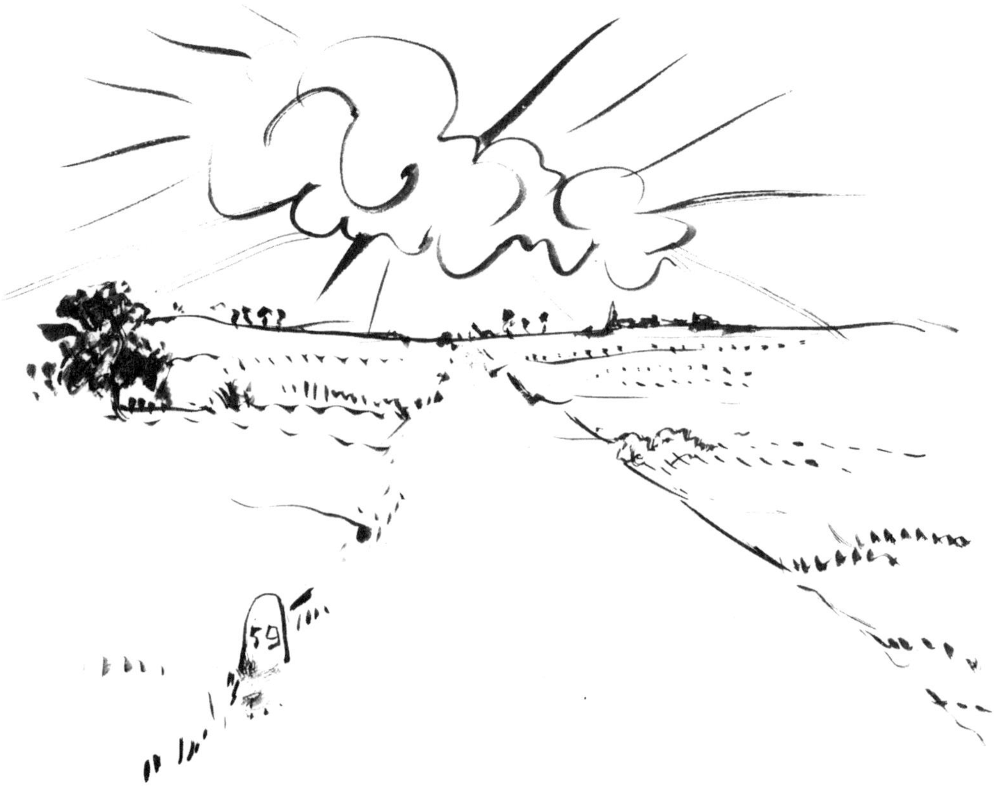

Dordrecht to Rotterdam

Of that short drive from Dordrecht to Rotterdam I remember nothing save that the car ran, glided rather, gently and smoothly, as though freed from the restraints of gravity. It was a delightful sensation, not exactly of leaping, nor of skating, but with something of each. She swept me along so light-heartedly that I felt equally buoyant myself: it was so smooth and swift that she might have been running as fast as she could along the road with bare feet.

Plutocrats and plover's eggs

One evening in Rotterdam I was taken to a club where I was assured, so they told me, of a warm welcome. The club members – local shipowners, bankers and business men – were all gathered in a big room. There were seats with small tables all around the sides, but the middle of the room was empty, the centre lights reflected in the mirror-like parquet floor. Each place was occupied, silently, by a drinker with a glass of beer before him; and above each drinker was a little cloud of smoke, all these clouds feeding the pall that hung over the whole room, its edges curling away into the bluish gloom. The smoke was emitted by the long pipes that the drinkers were puffing at intermittently. Every now and then there would be raps on the marble, punctuated by smacking of lips, shuffling of feet, hawking and coughing; then a flow of guttural speech, to which the others would listen patiently before drowning the final words in a general chorus of laughter.

My two neighbours spoke to me occasionally in low voices. One had a face cooked by wind and sun to the colour of terracotta and a thick collar of yellowish beard around his neck like a scarf. The other was a tiny old man who spent most of his time hoisting himself up so that his tiny chin came above the edge of the table. Now and then he removed his pipe and favoured me with the toothless grin of a very small child. He did practically nothing but smile. My friend informed me that he was one of the richest, most ruthless and luckiest speculators in the place, who had ruined more families than anyone else in Holland.

The evening wore on tediously, without incident,

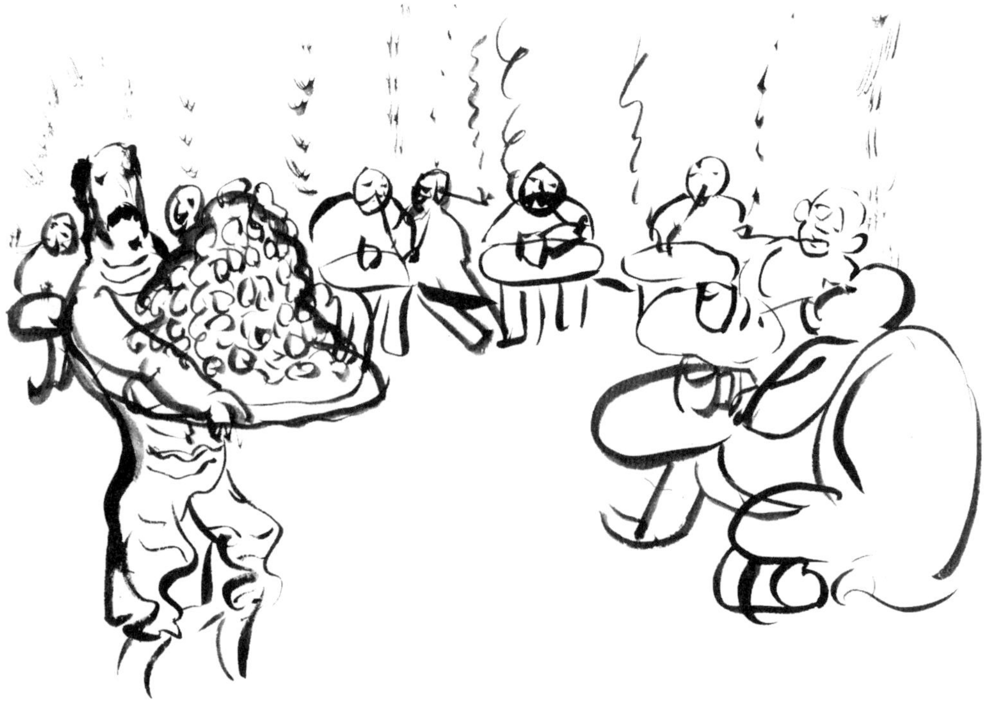

and without food. I found it hard to believe that so much desire for lucre, all the passions of finance, could be concealed behind those placid faces.

Late in the evening I was delighted to see an elegant tray carried in by a manservant in livery. Upon the tray was piled a pyramid-shaped hillock of plovers' eggs.

In a trice the hillock was demolished. The shells of the eggs were hurriedly torn off by dozens of fingers, with the sound that might have been made by a horde of rats.

The pleasure that I should have had, on my own, in savouring the salty whites and slightly muddy yolks was somewhat spoiled by the mute but embarrassing curiosity with which my fellow-eaters stared at me. And it proved to be a one-course meal.

It was after this meal that a voice from behind a flowing, white beard formally addressed me. It was a speech, delivered in French but a French embroidered with expressions that must have been left behind by the armies of Louis XIV. What I said in reply was amiably received. My neighbour on the right shook me warmly by the hand, while the little old man on my left smiled broadly. It was only afterwrds, as we were leaving, that I learnt from my friend that I had spoken much too fast and that the Dutchmen, even those who were most familiar with the language, had understood absolutely nothing of what I had said.

The half-open door

Thus far in our journey – and it is painful for a Frenchman to admit it – we had enjoyed no adventures (of an amatory nature) in hotels. Gerald B., the most travelled member of our party, and an Englishman into the bargain, maintained that they never occur.

'No. Absolutely never. Except of course what can happen to anybody in the street or in a night club. . . .'

But one evening after dinner in The Hague, he confessed he had been mistaken; and that adventures sometimes did take place in hotels. And after some initial reluctance, he told us his story.

He had returned to his hotel at about five o'clock and was surprised to find the door of his room half-open. He was even more surprised, when he walked in, to see, in the wardrobe mirror, a girl removing her chemise.

Higher and higher it rose, uncovering hips, then
waist, then shoulder blades, at which
stage it paused, until finally, with
great care so as not to
disarrange her

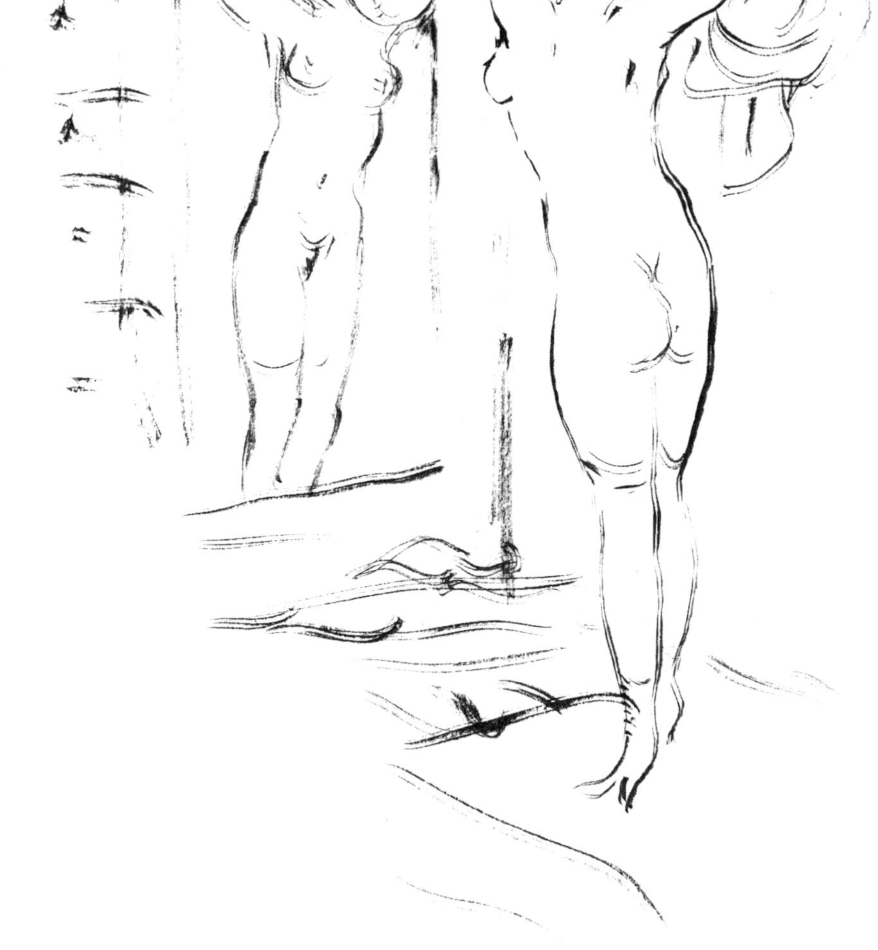

blonde hair, the owner lifted it clear. On hearing someone at the door, the unclad lady turned instinctively, and her face reddened.

'Monsieur, M-m-monsieur!' she cried, though not particularly loudly or angrily, her fingers fumbling with the filmy material and her rings becoming entangled in the lace. But never once, while struggling with the frothy cloud of batiste, did she succeed in veiling her bare breasts. Her body was ivory white, quite dazzling, except for the waist, where the tight lacing had cut what looked like bites and pinch marks in the flesh, and the legs, diaphanously sheathed in a pair of black openwork silk stockings.

Our friend closed and bolted the door.

'Monsieur! Oh, Monsieur!' she breathed, her voice trembling. Or did it?

He stole closer to the mirror which, far from affording a cloak for the lady's modesty, only made her look the more undressed.

'No please! No, no, don't please! . . . I . . . I . . . Please go away!'

Suppliant arms are weak. Our friend grasped her round the waist and drew her towards a bed littered with dresses, underwear, gloves and other miscellaneous garments, which he sent flying without a word; while the lady managed only 'M-monsieur, M-m-monsieur . . .', her entreaties dying away.

Soon he became aware of an answering pressure, of caresses responding to his. And of a muffled voice growing stronger, gasping, panting, then subsiding as in a swoon. 'Oh, my darling . . . my darling!'

Gerald was still chuckling when he returned to his room next door, where he sank into a chair and dozed until dinner.

'You must believe that I mistook the room,' he

remarked on concluding his tale. 'But what about her? How was it her door was open at that particular moment?'

We were lingering over our cigars and about to make some humorous aside to Gerald when his face suddenly went red – as red as the blushing lady with the chemise. He was not the only one to blush, however. A couple was entering the dining room; the girl cannot have been more than twenty-five, blonde, glittering with jet jewellery and blushing furiously. She paused uncertainly and grasped her billowing, green gauze shawl more tightly around her to increase her composure. Her partner was much older, tall, burly, fat, bald and unhealthy-looking. His disagreeable face had a shifty look about it; his hips were fat like those of an old woman and he waddled ridiculously as he followed the girl into the room. A dark purple carnation wilted in the button-hole of his dinner-jacket.

'Go on then my dear!' he said harshly, in Russian.

The table next to ours carried a basket of red roses and the head waiter hovered around the new arrivals, guiding them towards it. But the lady was clearly reluctant to sit there. She turned her head pointedly towards the other end of the room where, through some open French windows, was contrived a winter garden with palm trees and a fountain issuing from a pile of cardboard rocks, covered by some depressed-looking ferns, the whole effect inadequately lit by a candelabrum.

'No, it's not worth it,' urged the husband. 'Do get on with it, we're in a draught . . .'

At first he insisted upon her taking the chair which faced our table, but a short, sharp word from his wife obliged the colossus to be quiet and drop his florid head. He stood back and allowed her to take the other chair, and hide her blushes from us.

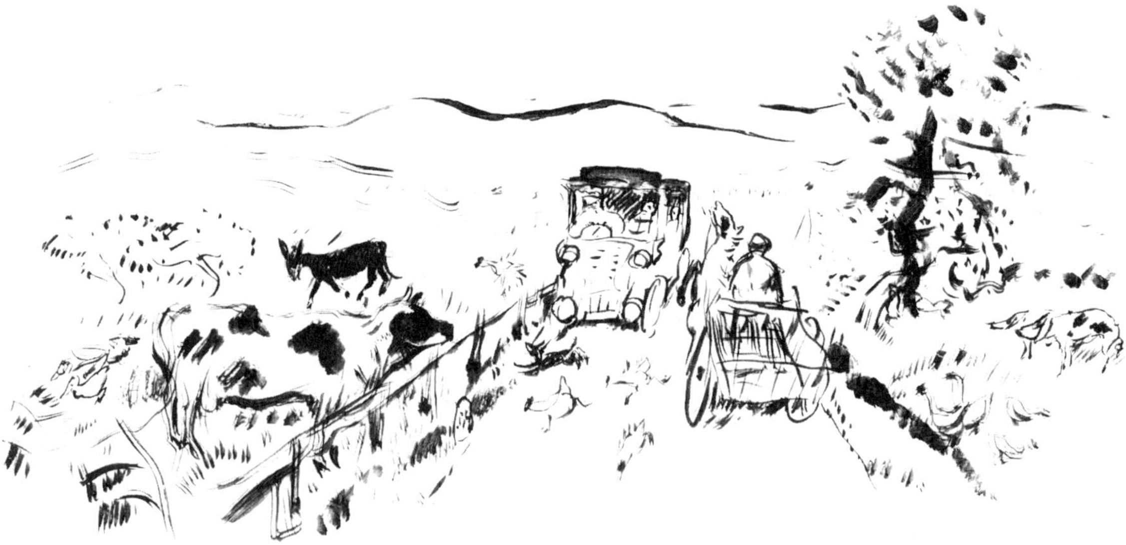

Animal life on the roads

This spring, bound for Grenoble via the Grands-Goulets, we were held up a few kilometres beyond Pont-en-Royans by a flock of at least two thousand sheep being driven to their high pastures, and had to trail behind them all the way to Villard de Lans. The shepherds, far from assisting us, seemed greatly amused by our discomfiture; and the sheepdogs, following their masters' example, not only revealed an almost human perverseness in their refusal to disperse the flock but added insult to injury by turning round and barking at us.

I raged inwardly as our poor car, reduced to a crawl, groaned its way forward, overheating and smoking to such an extent that I feared for the cylinders.

My love for animals is positively neurotic, even misanthropic. Their suffering fills me with horror. But I would willingly have driven full tilt into that flock with all the power of our forty horses and ground those sheep into bloody mincemeat, had I not reflected on the serious consequences it might entail for the vehicle and for ourselves. I contented myself with letting out savage blasts on the horn. The criminal thought, struck me that the creatures might be seized with panic and run mad, leaping over the parapet to be dashed to pieces at the foot of the precipice and carried away by the torrent.

Nothing of the sort happened. The hooting, though magnified by echoes from the mountainsides, made no impression on the animals, accustomed, no doubt, to the rumblings of avalanches. The mass of piteously bleating sheep seemed to be airborne, visibly moving only at the edges, yet the pattering of thousands of feet sounded like a continuous roll of thunder – or, indeed, like a motor car with serious engine trouble. And flocks of sheep raise just as much dust as cars, and do as much damage to the roads.

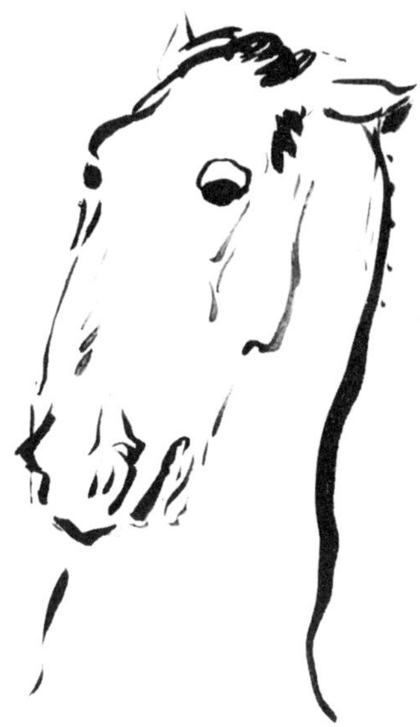

The manner in which different animals react to passing cars is a reflection of their character and degree of intelligence. The horse, for example, which Buffon infuriatingly called 'man's noblest conquest', is plain stupid. The horse is frightened by smells, by colours, by light, by shade, by its own shadow. It is scared by scraps of paper, bits of shiny glass, a gleam of moonlight in a puddle or a wisp of fog drifting across the road. It suffers from every kind of phobia, including autophobia. When a car comes really close, it shies, rears, breaks its harness and tips everything, carriage and occupants alike, into the ditch.

Like the hare, which is dangerous to no one but itself and does not haunt the roads, the horse endures the

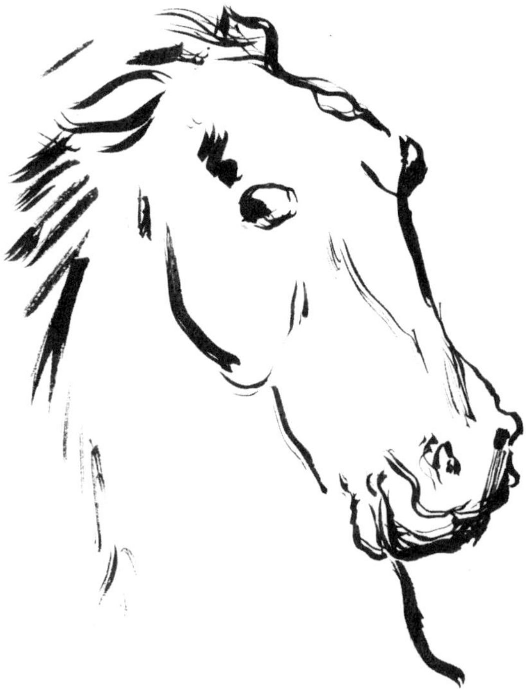

physical handicap
of being unable to look straight
ahead, only to the right or left, like politicians.
In order to walk without bumping into anything or hurting itself it must be unable to see at all. Blindfold him and he will plod sleepily around without stopping, turning the wheel of a merry-go-round, for instance, hour after hour. No other animal on the road – pedestrians and cyclists included – is so dangerous or so to be mistrusted. Every

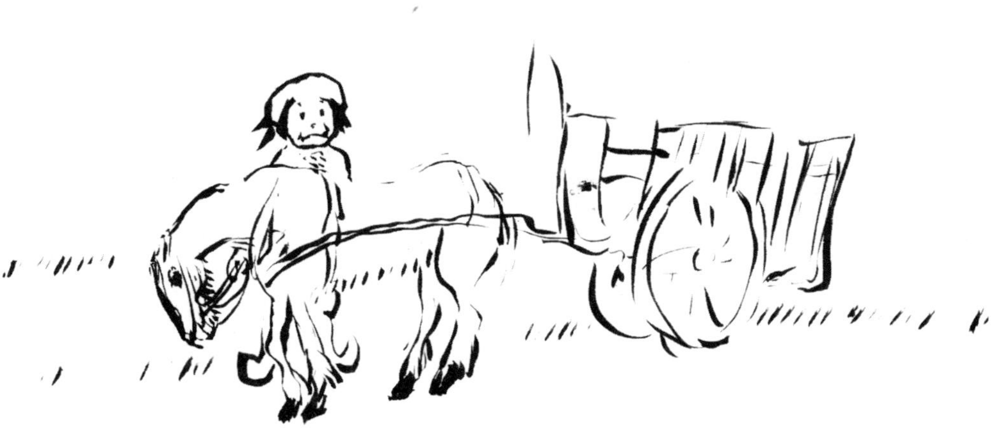

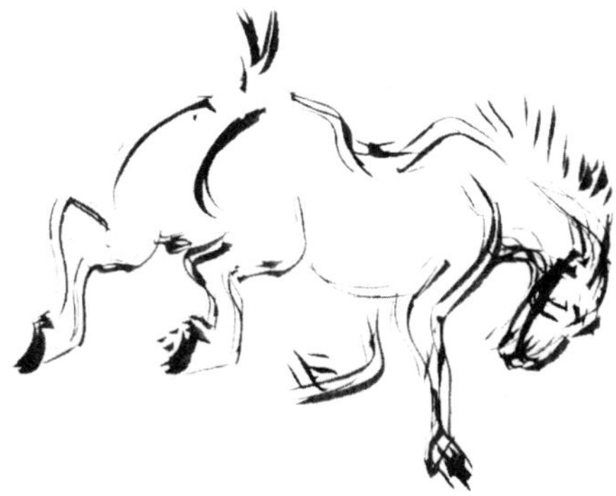

time I meet one of
these perilous idiots I slow
down or stop, for one never knows what
mischief, what homicidal thoughts, may be running
through its mind . . .

This same fear is also experienced by some humans . . . peasants in the countryside around Morbihan and other Breton-speaking parts have a particular fear of the motor car, regarding it as the work of Old Nick himself. The moment one of them spots an oncoming car, he starts muttering prayers; if on foot he kneels down, clasping together trembling hands, and invokes St. Yves, who bestows riches, and St. Tugen, who cures rabies. As yet there are no saints in Brittany who protect against the automobile.

Cows and oxen are on a par with horses; but as with townsfolk and country people, cattle bear a more intellectual resemblance to the slower-witted but more sensible peasants. A couple of cows or bullocks on their way to the farmyard or abattoir look quite funny lumbering ahead of the car, wagging their great rumps and swishing their silly tails. They can continue some distance like this but even a herd of calves, under such pressure, will eventually

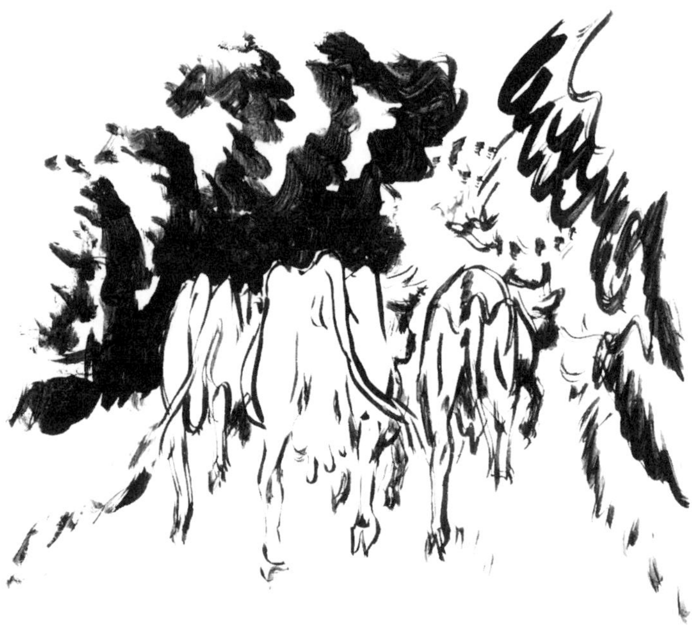

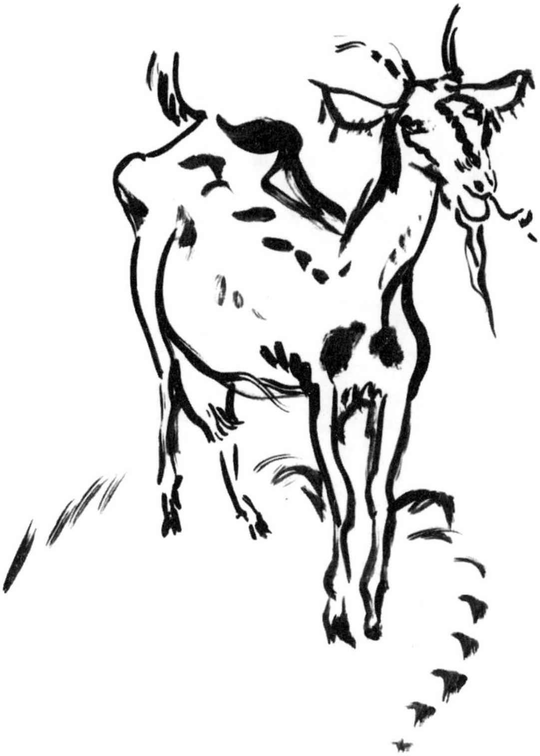

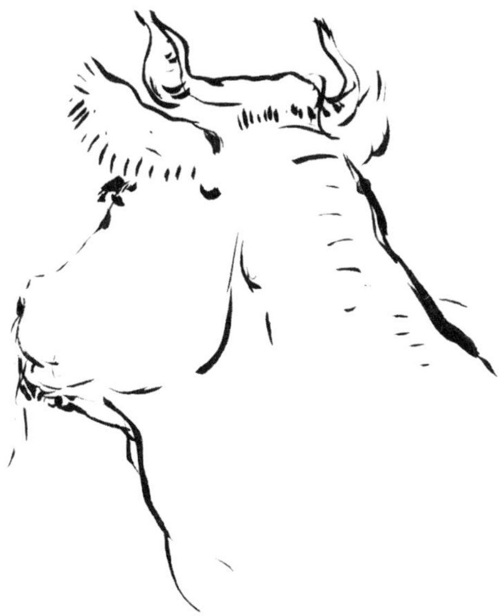

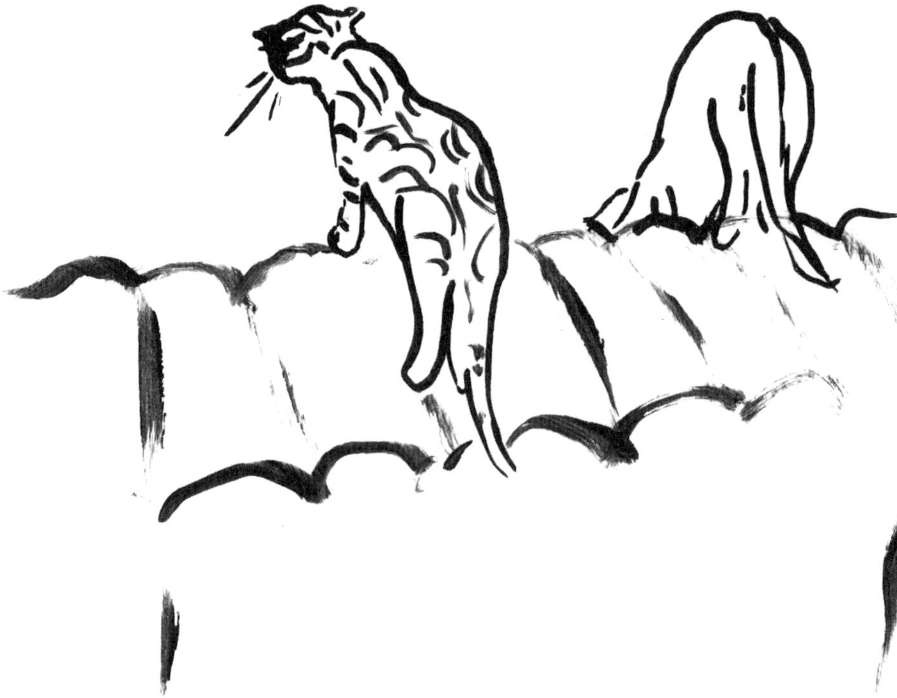

turn down a side road or through a gap in the hedge into a field, and watch curiously but with a friendly air as you drive past. They only lose their heads completely when a horse disturbs them and infects them with its stupid fears.

Goats, so highly strung that their milk is said to give some children convulsions, only panic if tethered with their young. Then they tug helplessly at their bonds and charge around the stake as far as the chain will allow them, capering, tumbling and tossing their horns. Once freed, they climb nimbly up the bank, seemingly unconcerned, to browse safely on tender shoots in the undergrowth.

Good theme for a lecture on the educational virtues of freedom.

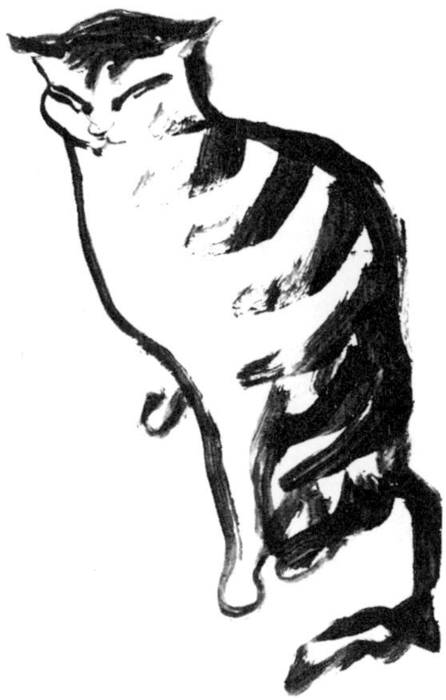

We all know the deeply meditative nature of cats. Right from the outset they saw the motor car as a new danger, and straight away, quietly and without fuss, they steered clear of it. You don't meet many on the open road, which doesn't suit their mysterious comings and goings; they prefer dark, bosky places. Now and then they emerge cautiously from a hedge with a live fieldmouse in their mouth. As a rule, however, they just sit on village doorsteps and watch the passing traffic with the same deceptively absent-minded gaze with which they follow the flight of a butterfly.

Few indeed are the drivers who catch them out.

Piglets, so pink and so pretty, try to keep pace with the car, galloping joyously along the verge. It is one of the pleasures of motoring to see these delightful little creatures chasing one another and pursuing us as in a charming nursery frieze, snout down, ears flapping, tail wagging – as plump and chubby-cheeked as cherubs, only pinker.

Poor little fellows! Sad to think that all that youthful enthusiasm, all that bouncing gaiety will end up, quite soon, in the sausage-machine.

So much for piglets. But let's be fair to the old porkers as well. You don't see much of them. Contrary to what is usually supposed, these animals are very clean and only wallow in muddy pools because they are tormented by a desire to bathe. The older pigs don't haunt the roads, except when returning from market. Sometimes you see them beside ditches or ponds, splashing voluptuously in the water. But do they really enjoy it? They are good-natured and indulgent, like all fat people, and they seem to say:

'Really! Don't you think we wouldn't prefer a nice bath
with lots of clean water, scented with benzoin? We dirty
old pigs do nothing but dream of soapsuds,
almond paste, massage, pedicure.
. . . But all we get is this.
It has to do.'

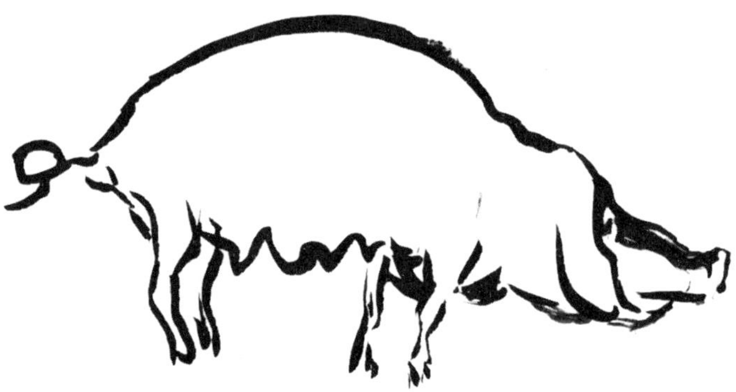

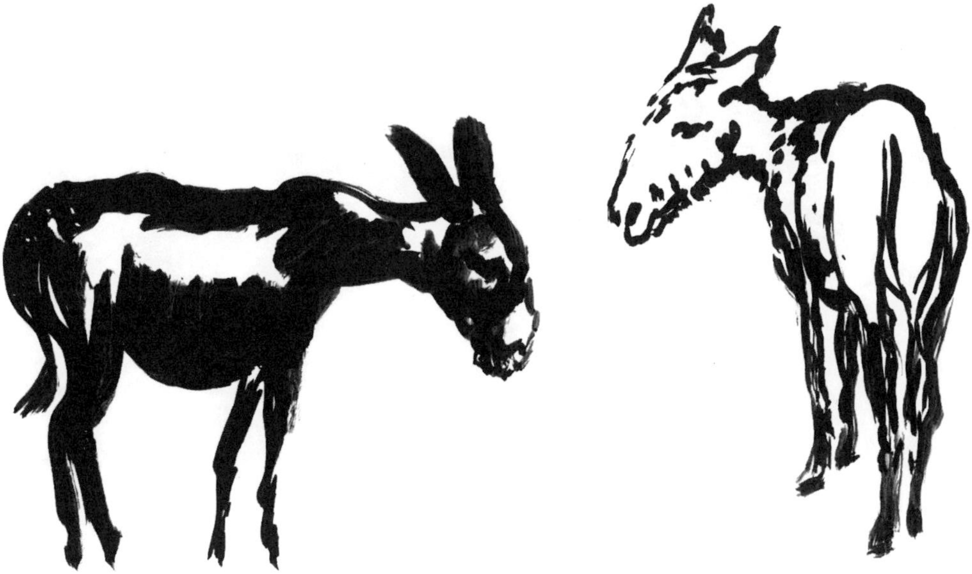

If, very occasionally, they are run over crossing the road, they certainly take their revenge. There is no case on record where the car has not overturned on impact with that mass of meat and fat, making a horrible mess of man and pig.

The donkey is no less trammelled, nor the mule . . . but what a difference. How well they judge their masters' stupidity, their ridiculous whims, their contradictory orders. And how bravely they resist them – with the courage of common sense! They detest incoherence, and will respond only to whatever is logical and tangible, which makes them seem impossible to train. In contrast to the horse's manifestations of fright, all that noisy repertoire of shying, kicking and bolting, the donkey passes demurely by with that sensible little trot and eyes the machine without fear – quite unimpressed.

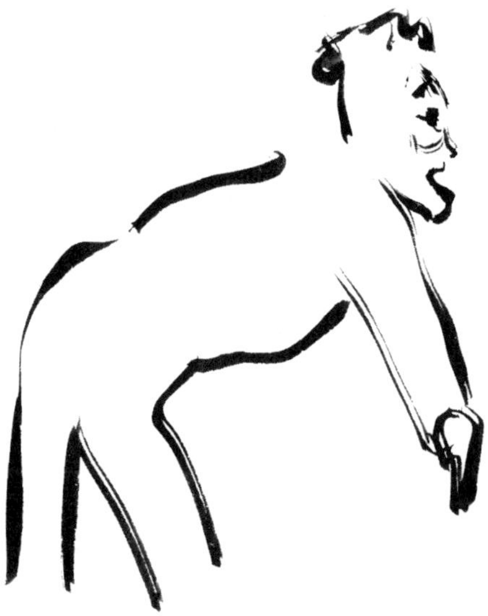

The dog has two disadvantages: its faithfulness and the stupidity of its master. It trusts its owner right up to the moment of being put down, and demonstrates its idiotic devotion for the last time by thanking him with a dying glance and licking his hands. . . .

Dogs will dash out at a car to protect their master and his possessions against fancied dangers. They are always barking at something or somebody, or at nothing. I can't believe their celebrated sense of smell misleads them to the extent of mistaking a car radiator for a friend's backside. No. Dogs are clearly less concerned

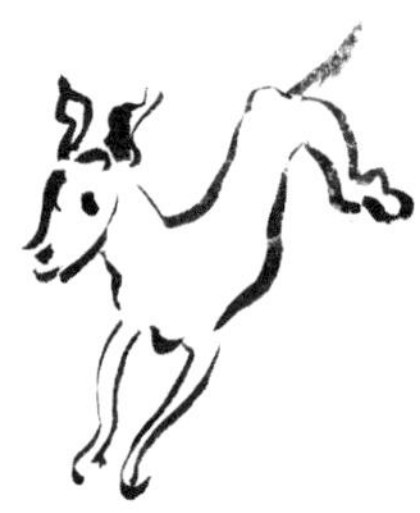

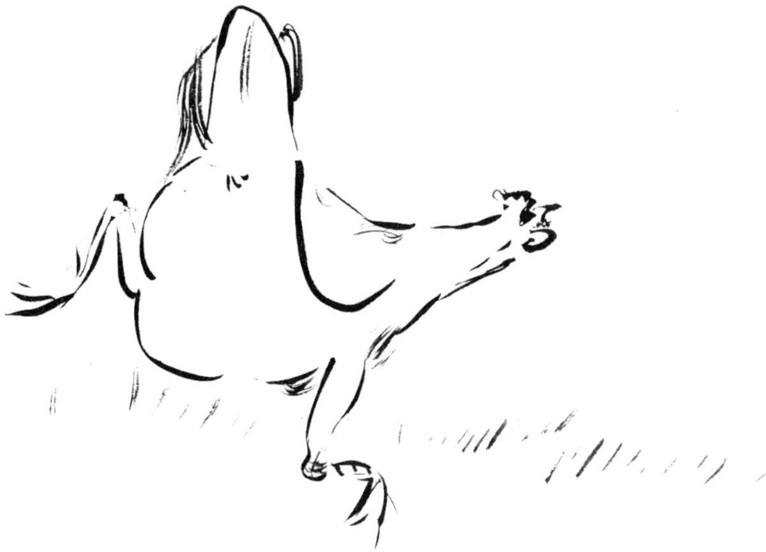

with avoiding cars than with
charging them and thus having an excuse
to bark. This annoying habit often gets them run over.

Nine times out of ten the owner is entirely to blame. No sooner is the dog safely settled on one side of the road than its master calls – in that same silly, bossy voice that mothers use to summon their children in similar circumstances. And the dog, which enjoys being stroked more than a man and being whipped more than a woman, leaps up and bounds across. Has he recognised the danger? No matter. He obeys because he is faithful, and because he is faithful he gets run over.

Hens are absurd. Nowhere in the whole of the animal kingdom is there a better example of mental instability. Greed is their ruling passion, far greater than lechery. Pigs compared with them are sober and chaste. No carnivore is more bloody, no hawk more rapacious than these little monsters, whose head is all beak, whose round eyes are coldly cruel, and who are clad in the prettiest dresses imaginable. They get themselves run over for the sake of one last peck at anything in the road, a horse-dropping, a cowpat, maybe only a stone.

They seem to cross the road, for no one is calling them from the other side, simply for the fun of confronting a car radiator. If they avoid the car, it is only to crash into a telegraph pole, a tree or a wall, or to get entangled in a hedge. When running, they stretch out their necks so far, beak open, feathers ruffled, that you expect them to continue on all fours until at the last second danger rekindles the racial instinct and momentarily transforms a piece of poultry back into a bird. Once safe, a grain of corn or an insect on a blade of grass makes them forget the entire episode. They just peck and peck. They are like the woman in the Scriptures who arose from table, wiped her lips and said, 'I have not eaten.'

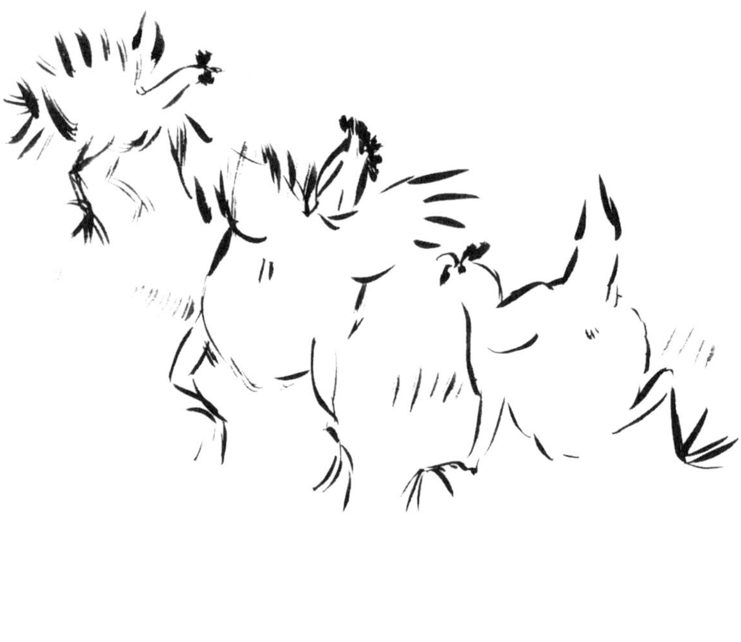

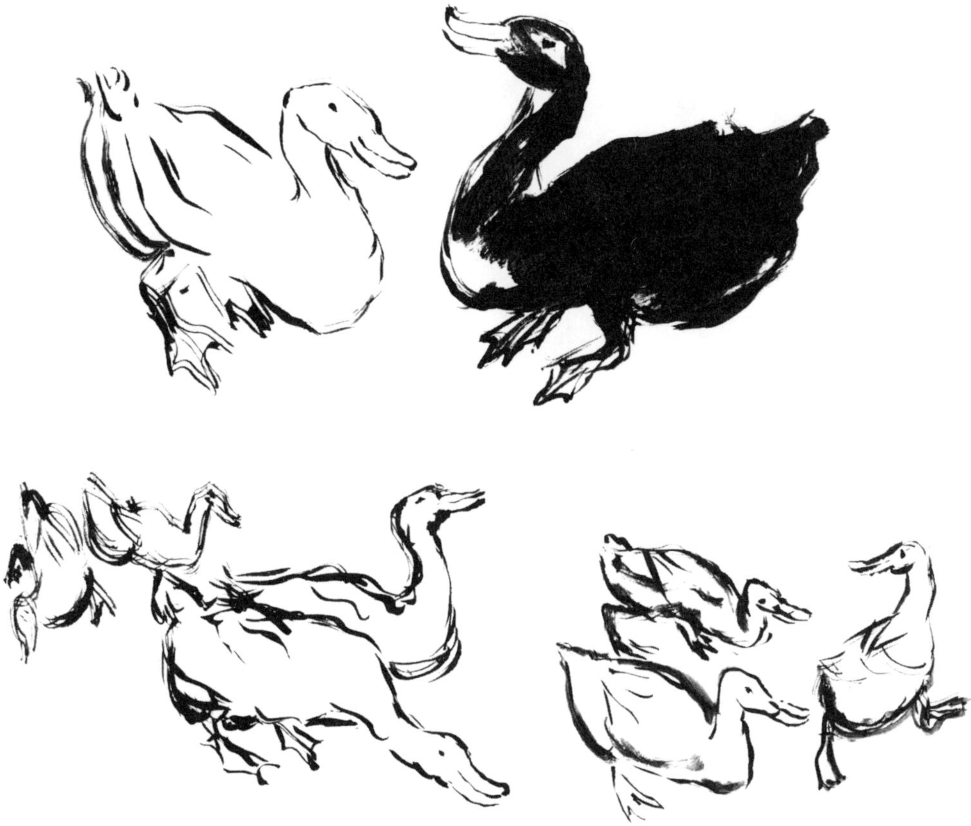

Ducks are much more talented. Although deprived of defences by having been removed from the streams and ponds on which they are so gracefully ornamental, they cope very well. They waddle in humiliated little groups off to one side, never taking the crown of the road, knowing quite well they have nothing to fear if they stick to the edge. Ducks know a lot of things. They are practically never run over.

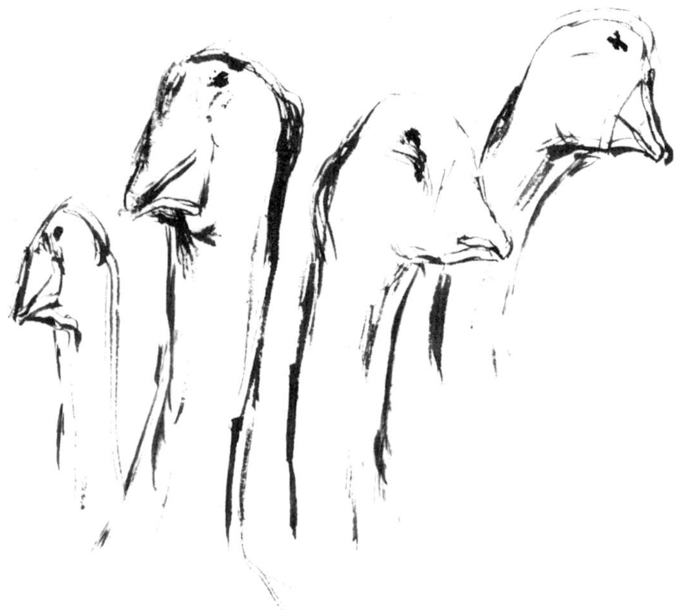

The same goes for turkeys, for they are well guarded. Turkeys have no truck with the riffraff on the roads; their special enclosures resemble academies where they puff themselves up, like poets and artists, at their ease.

I would like to make a special plea, however, for geese. These illustrious creatures certainly merited the honour of guarding the Capitol. They have inspired Japanese artists to paint admirable masterpieces, and their decorative possibilities have been exploited on bath-taps, water hydrants, wash-basins and Empire-style armchairs.

Their only black mark – which they bear with ironic fortitude – is to furnish the quills with which men write so many lies and so much nonsense. On the other hand we have to thank them for the quilt and for *pâté de foie gras*.

On the road, whenever a car goes by, geese line up one behind the other on the verge, without a trace of panic, dignified despite their waddling gait, and not afraid to speak their minds to the strangers who disturb them but do not impress them.

I have never driven past a flock of geese without feeling embarrassed, humiliated by their contempt. Their hissing intimidates me because it is ridicule, not bad language. Rudeness one can ignore, but mockery hurts.

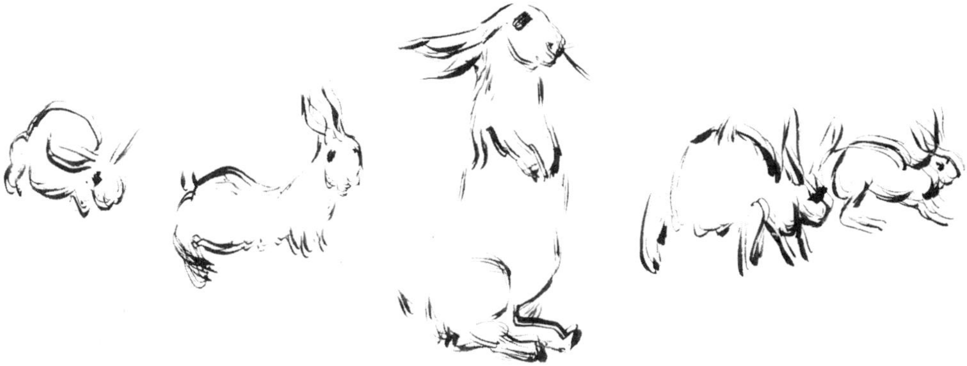

In Germany, driving through the woods after dark, I have often sighted rabbits – in enormous numbers – but I have never caught or run over a single one. They were charming – even though German – as they played on the road, brightly lit by the headlamps. They frisked about, held little meetings here and there, and made off, with a flourish of their white powder-puff tails, only when the car was almost on top of them.

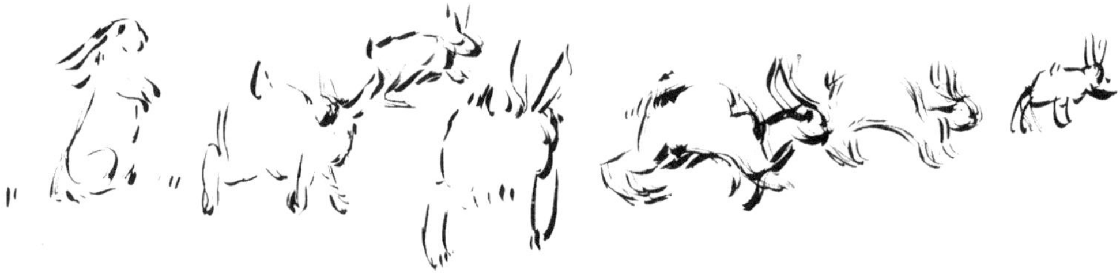

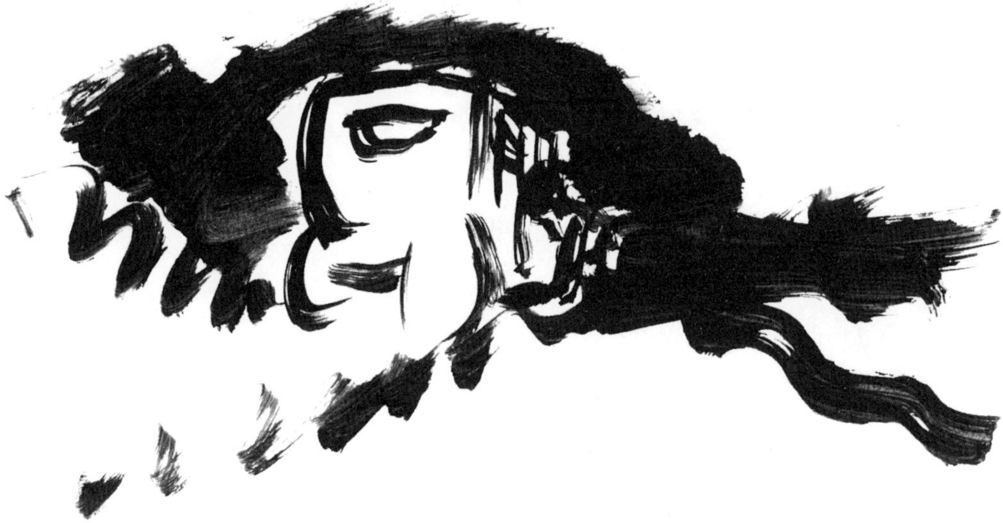

Martians

It was pitch dark. Not a soul
on the road, not the ghost of a car. All village
lights were out, not a house alive. The dogs had
stopped barking. We paced up and down to keep warm,
our shadows immense in the headlamps. Brossette was
sweating over a puncture. The discarded cover and tube
lay in the ditch. We felt helpless and very hungry.
Eventually he finished changing the tyre and we
set off. As we climbed a very steep hill a cold light
appeared on the horizon and gradually filled the sky.
Suddenly it burst over the hilltop, vast, dazzling,

overwhelming, and bore down on us. It roared, spat thunder, and in a cloud of golden dust swept past, carrying with it shouts, laughter, the blast of a horn, nothing visible but a glint of brasswork and some wisps of veil the colour of the moon. Like a flash it was gone, restoring the darkness which it had briefly torn to shreds. . . . Then the sky lit up again and there was another blinding whirlwind, leaving only blackness in its wake . . . and another . . . and another.

Suddenly our own headlights picked out the silhouette of an enormous car, unlit and lifeless, with two men bending over it. I say men; but maybe they were Martians. They had no shape, being shrouded in long sack-like coats from head to foot, and when one of them straightened up, waving his arms, nothing was visible of his face but a small white triangle, like a mask, beneath the metal frames of his goggles. The 628-E8 came to a halt.

The head of the smaller man was buried in the car's gigantic bonnet. The other man, tall and thin, was holding a steel rod. He enquired, in a Russian accent, whether I could possibly lend him a pin, a tie-pin, say, preferably made of gold. Puzzled, I eventually gathered that it was a matter of unclogging the headlight's acetylene burner. But why gold? At that moment a motorcyclist, like some monstrous insect, brushed past him so close that I expected, at the very least, to find the man's coat had been whipped off; but he just dusted himself off and laughed, gazing after the motorcyclist as if regretting that there had been no time to ask for a gold tie-pin.

They tried to detain us no longer and we left them by the roadside, the taller man waving us goodbye, the other not speaking a word or raising his
head from the
engine. . . .

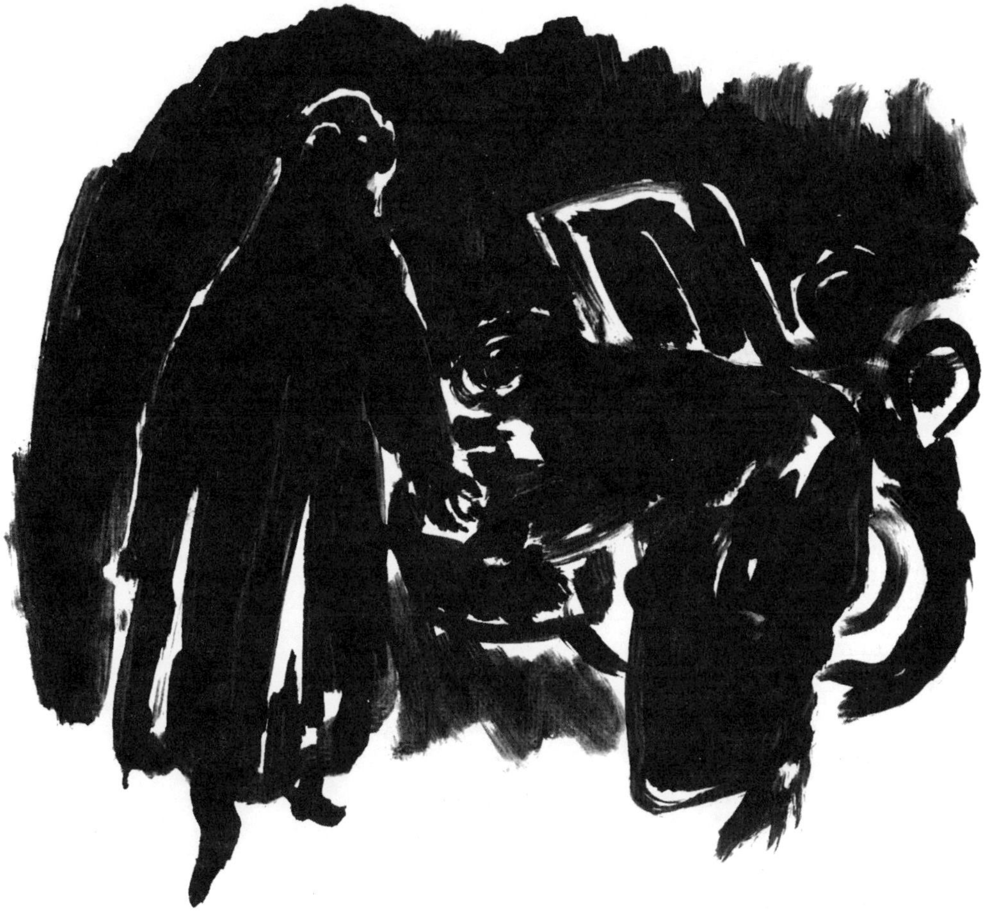

Cyclists and motorists

The moment a man – no matter how charming – bestrides a bicycle, he becomes a horse, with all the whims, the crazy cavortings and mad prancings of that creature – but how much more dangerous! For as a rule he is a voter . . . and thus privileged he never bothers to keep to his side of the road. Does not everything belong to him – the road, the career of his chosen candidate, the majority of the government he supports? He picks on everyone and on everything, pedestrians, carriages, motor cars, animals; he is the master, the sole master, of the road. Watch him, hands in pockets, cap on the back of his head, showing off, wobbling all over the place, doing spirals and zigzags for no reason except to get in the way. In the course of which manoeuvres, like the dog, he sometimes gets run over . . . in which case there is hell to pay, enormous damages, perhaps months in prison.

But if one cyclist is bad, he is nothing compared to a whole group. When they take the road, it's goodbye to everyone. You might as well go home.

I'd rather have those couple of thousand sheep in the gorges of the Grands-Coulets any day.

As for the motorist – surely he is the worst of all the animals on the road. I am aware of it myself. When standing on *terra firma* I quietly examine my conscience, and am horrified to realise that I am sometimes that very creature. . . .

When I am in the car, possessed by speed, humanitarian feelings drain away. I begin to feel obscure

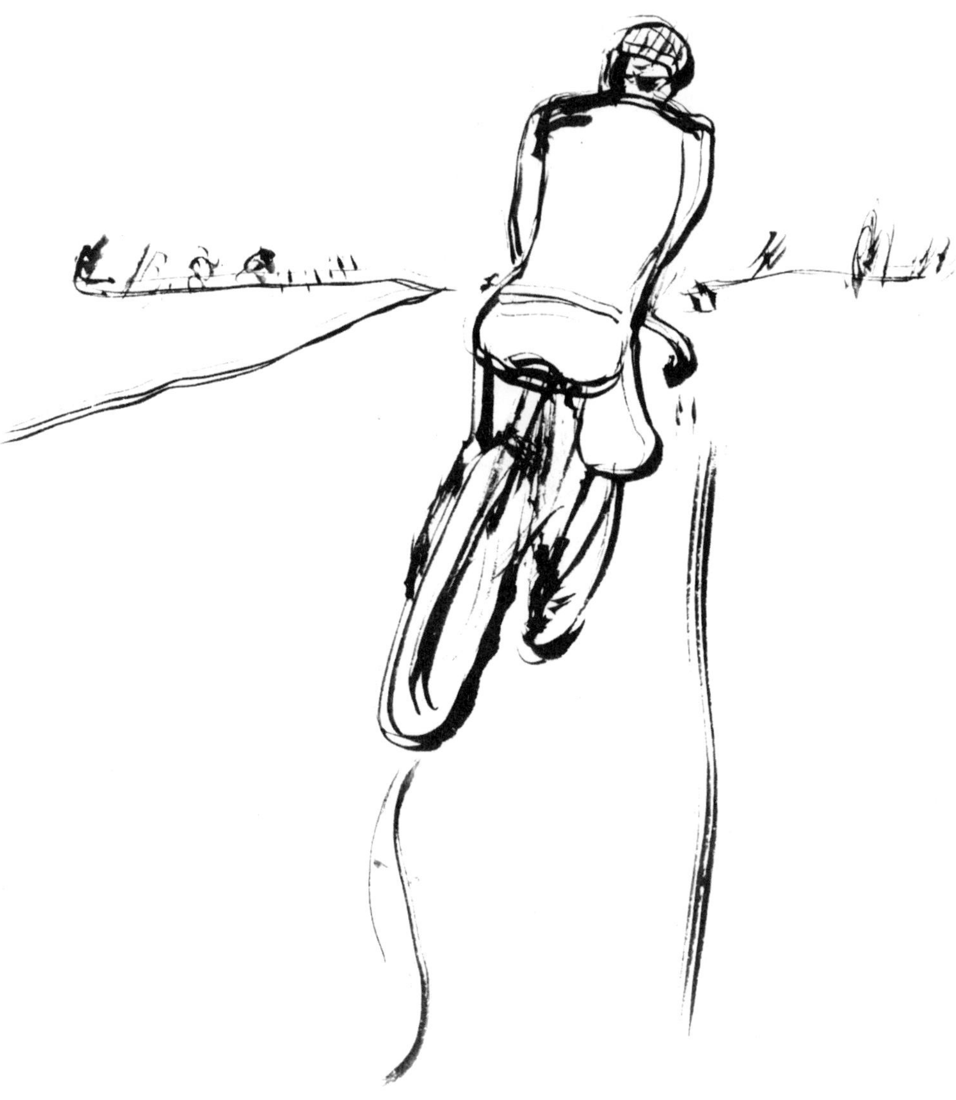

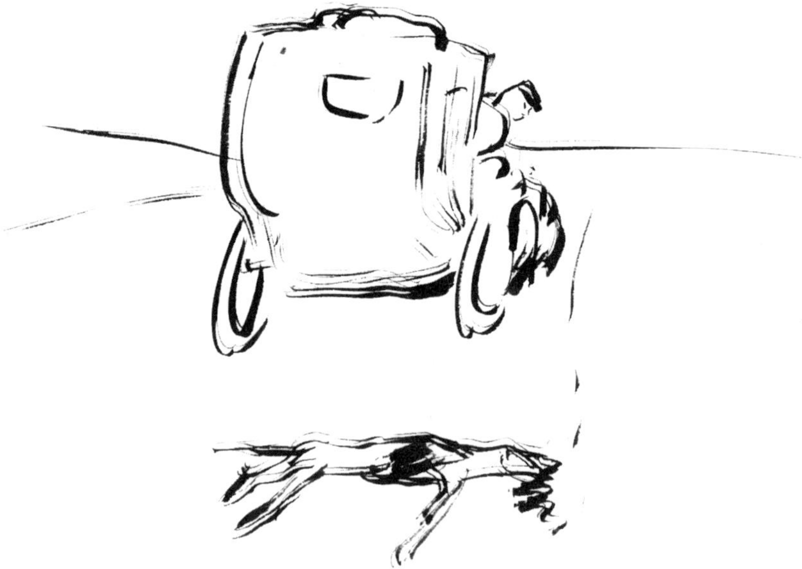

stirrings of hatred and an idiotic sense of pride. No longer am I a miserable specimen of humanity, but a prodigious being in whom are embodied – no, please don't laugh – Elemental Splendour and Power. And given I am the Wind, the Storm, the Thunderbolt, imagine with what contempt I view the rest of humanity from the vantage-point of my car. . . . Yet not much of an Element really, which a cart across the road can bring to a humiliating halt, or a piece of stone send flying into a ditch.

Never mind, never mind. Out of my way!

How frustrating, how thoroughly disheartening it is that these pig-headed, obstructive villagers, whose hens, dogs and sometimes children I mow down, fail to appreciate that I represent Progress and universal happiness. I intend to bring them these benefits in spite of themselves, even if they don't live to enjoy them!

A tragic accident

One day, driving from La Ferté-sous-Jouarre to Meaux, I saw a group of people behaving strangely. One of them signalled me to stop.

A motor car, twisted and bent, blocked the road. Near by, on the grass verge, lay a little peasant girl, twelve years old at most, her chest crushed, her face bloody. Bending over her was a woman, trying to resuscitate her.

'Madeleine! My little Madeleine!' she wailed.

I went and examined the child, then administered injections of ether and caffeine into the thorax, alas in vain.

'She is dead,' I told the mother.

Her cries became heartrending. Then the owner of the upturned car appeared, quite uninjured, although a powdering of dust had blackened his fair beard. He addressed the mother:

'Don't distress yourself, my good woman. No doubt what has happened is regrettable, and it would be better had I not killed your child. I sympathise with you in your grief. However, there is a bright side. Since I'm insured it's of little consequence to me . . . . Consider, after all, that there can be no progress in the world without some cost in human lives . . . think of the railways, and submarines. And it's obvious, is it not, that motoring represents one such example of progress, perhaps the greatest, in this admirable age. True, it killed your daughter, but remember that it affords a livelihood to two thousand workmen in France alone! And think of the future, my good woman. Soon a system of public transport will spring up; all these small isolated communities will be in touch with the great centres of activity. New trades will arise, new sources of wealth, an undreamed-of new life . . . . So tell yourself that your daughter has sacrificed herself for all this. She is a martyr, a martyr to progress. And you will soon find consolation. Now I am going to take your name and address, and I shall write to my insurance company this very evening. It's a first-rate company. You will receive an offer of compensation, in keeping, naturally, with your social status. Anyway, don't worry, they'll treat you reasonably . . . . I'm the one to be pitied. Look at my car. I shall have to take the train back to Paris, which is always humiliating for a true motorist like me. I too take comfort, for I remind myself that I am working for progress and the universal good. Goodbye!'

I could not bear the thought of so perfect a motorist travelling by train. I offered him a seat in my car.

And while the mother continued to sob over her daughter's corpse, he remarked, settling down snugly beside me, 'It's not easy to instil the true notion of progress into these poor folk. They're so . . . .'

He did not finish the sentence, perhaps mindful of that child's body by the roadside, which could so easily give him the lie. I said nothing. It was time to be off, and my own thoughts were confused. Did I too, as a motorist, stand for Progress and Happiness? I felt a bit frightened.

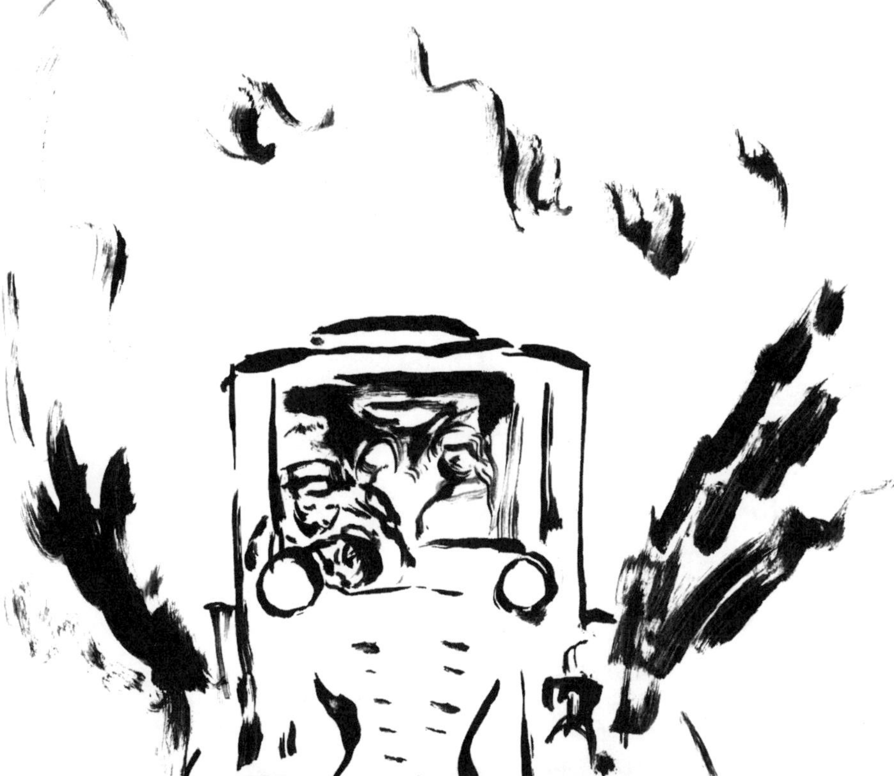

Along the Rhine

Readers will recall the unexpected ease with which we crossed the German frontier at Elten, and the benevolent customs man who stood in the road waving us goodbye. We were bound for Düsseldorf, you may remember . . . . And the smooth, dead straight road, with no bends or gradients, was an invitation to speed.

Not an obstruction of any kind, no dips in the road, no steep cambers – a road as well tended as a cycle-racing track. All the vehicles we passed kept scrupulously to the right, and the carters reined in their horses, waving us on in the most friendly fashion.

'What a pity we're in Germany, sir!'

'Why is that, Brossette?'

'Because I don't care for that lot at all . . . . And because it's a lovely road, sir, where we could do 90 kilometres an hour, even more, perhaps . . . .'

He was silent for a while, then: 'It's strange. Are you quite sure we're in Germany, sir?

'Positive! Don't you remember the frontier a little way back?'

He shrugged. 'Oh, that! Don't call that a frontier. Givet, yes, with all those forts, that's a real frontier, that is. But if you're sure . . . .

'Dirty, rotten country, all the same', he grumbled.

We continued driving at a leisurely rate. The 628-E8, however, was impatient. You could feel her quivering, champing the bit like an eager stallion, raring to go. It was as though she were tugging at the steering-wheel as a horse tugs at the reins. I saw from a village clock that it was half-past four and it was still 200 kilometres to Düsseldorf, which I wanted to reach before dark.

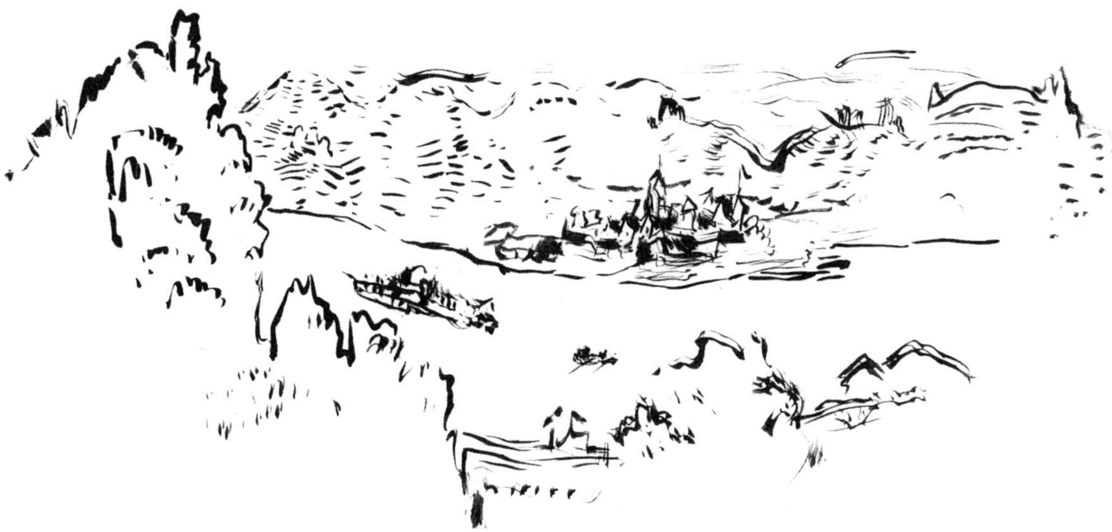

The air was cool,
the engine humming
nicely. 'Right, put your foot
down, Brossette! Let's see what she
can do.' And the good old CGV, freed from restraint,
leapt forward, eating up the road.

In a few minutes we reached Emmerich, where a powerful steamboat ferried us across the Rhine.

A little way beyond Krefeld we came up behind a spanking little pony and trap driven by a peasant girl. The pony took fright, laid back its ears and bolted. I stopped the car, but the terrified animal refused to calm down. Taking her life in her hands, the girl jumped awkwardly from the trap and tumbled into the road. I rushed to her rescue and helped her up. She was blonde, with a lovely complexion and very neatly dressed.

Once on her feet, she managed to smile and blurted out excuses: 'It's that naughty pony . . . . My goodness, he's silly! Scared of everything . . . . I'm so sorry.'

She had modestly lifted her skirt and discovered a slight graze on her knee. I found some peroxide in my first-aid kit and bathed the sore, which was hardly bleeding at all. She protested and giggled, 'It's quite all right, truly. Goodness, it does sting a bit!' Then she repeated, 'It's that blessed pony . . . . I really am sorry to have been so much trouble!'

Brossette had caught the pony and was soothing it with sweet talk.

As we handed the girl back into the trap, 'Thank you again, I'm most grateful', she said. Then, imploringly, 'Please, sir, don't talk about this, not to anyone . . . because if they got to hear of this at home, you know, they'd never, ever, let me drive to Krefeld on my own.' She picked up the reins. 'Gee up! Just you keep quiet, you silly thing . . . . I am so sorry . . . so sorry.' Half an hour later we were crossing the Rhine by the great bridge at Düsseldorf.

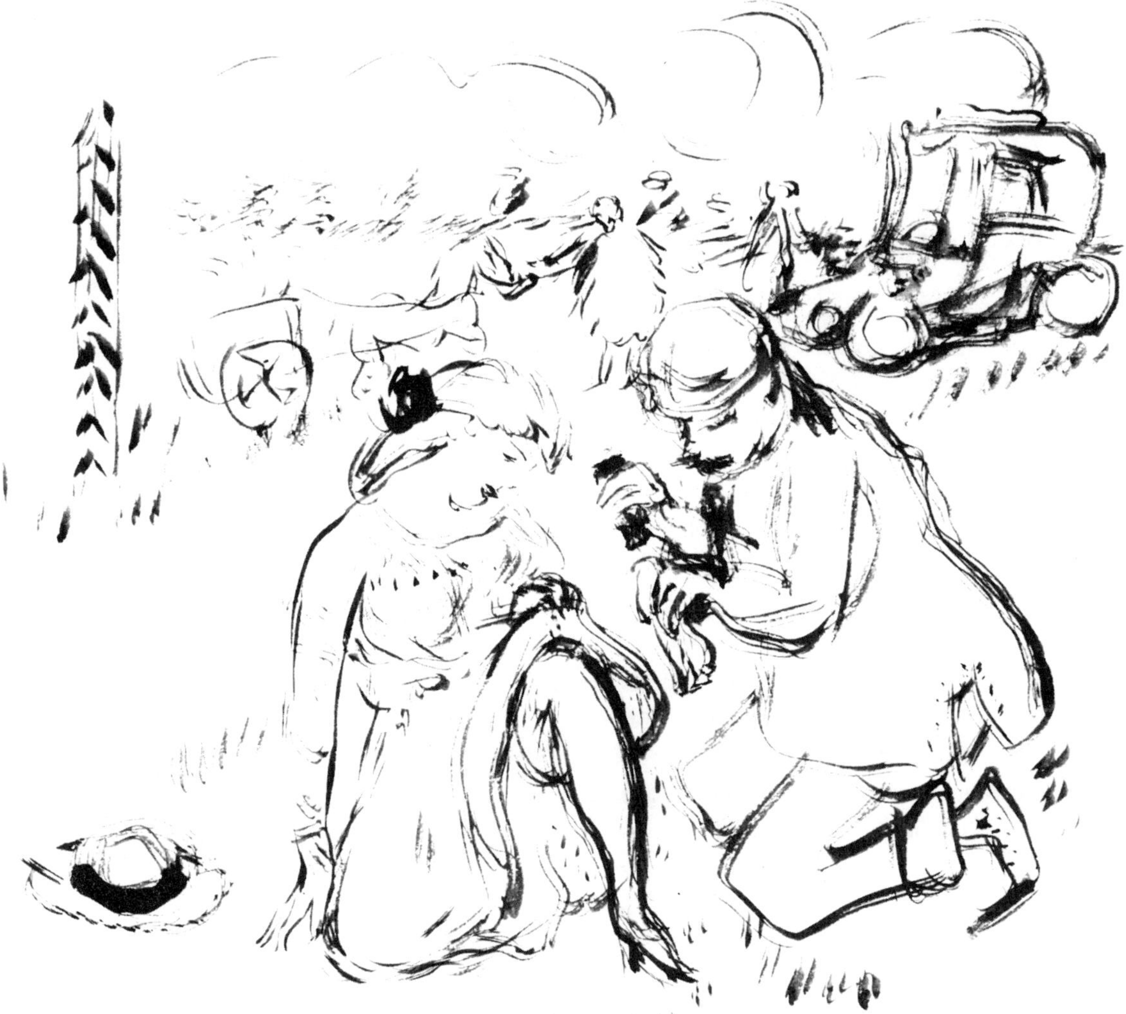

Modern-style

The Brandenburgerhof at Düsseldorf is one of those grand hotels, such as you find in the smallest German towns and which in France exist only in Paris and certain watering places, a new-fangled caravanserai in Western modern-style *(Art Nouveau)*, built by Belgians and Swiss for the comfort of the Americans and the English . . . . Sitting-rooms, vaguely Louis XV and Louis XVI, next door to ocean liner smoking-rooms. Everything round has become square, everything square has become round. What I mean to say is that nothing is round, or square, or oval, or oblong, or triangular, or vertical or horizontal. Everything twists and turns, curves first one way and then the other, winds and unwinds, for quite inexplicable reasons. All you see are festoons of gleaming copper, mouldings of coloured wood, ellipses of polychrome faïence, volutes of glazed earthenware, piers of embossed leather, and friezes of hairy water-lilies, angry poppies and sunflowers adorning the mouldings of columns, like parrots on their perches . . . . Larvae squat at the keyholes, embryos and tadpoles clamber and slither in slimy waves over doors, windows and drawers. The chimney-pieces are bookcases, the bookcases are draught-screens, the draught-screens are cupboards, the cupboards are sofas. The electricity comes out of the floor as well as the ceilings, from crystal globes cut into the shape of dreamlike flowers or nightmare beasts; it runs, bumps, bowls, frisks, spins and cakewalks its way through chandeliers and lamps as in a mad St. Vitus' dance. The furniture looks as if it is drunk, and the balustrades of the balconies are held up by frenzied sarabands of question marks.

These sorts of hotel, with such repugnant decorative features, have at least one valuable asset: they offer the fastidious traveller the finest resources in the way of plumbing and hygiene . . . . I had to admit that here I was far from *la belle France* where almost everywhere, even in the big towns, the hotels jealously preserve the habit of our race, the hereditary taint by which a Frenchman can be recognised, far better than by his wit, namely uncleanliness.

I remember arriving one day at a town in the Morvan, where I stopped at a charming little hotel . . . and was horrified at the shameful condition of those intimate quarters, lined throughout with china tiles which, if the trademark was to be believed, came direct from England. I complained bitterly to the manager, who replied with a discouraged air, 'Ah, don't speak of it, Monsieur . . . .'

'Nonsense, that is precisely what I wish to do.'

'But it's not my fault, I assure you. It's those French people, who know so many things, they just don't know how to sh –. They are pigs, Monsieur.'

He flew into a rage. 'You've seen for yourself, I've put up notices, explaining how the things should be used, but it's no use. They even try to stand up on them. It's disgusting . . . .'

'Maybe,' he added optimistically, 'with all these sports – with motor cars – they'll learn to behave decently like everyone else. But there's a lot to be done, a lot to be done!'

'To be done differently,' I growled.

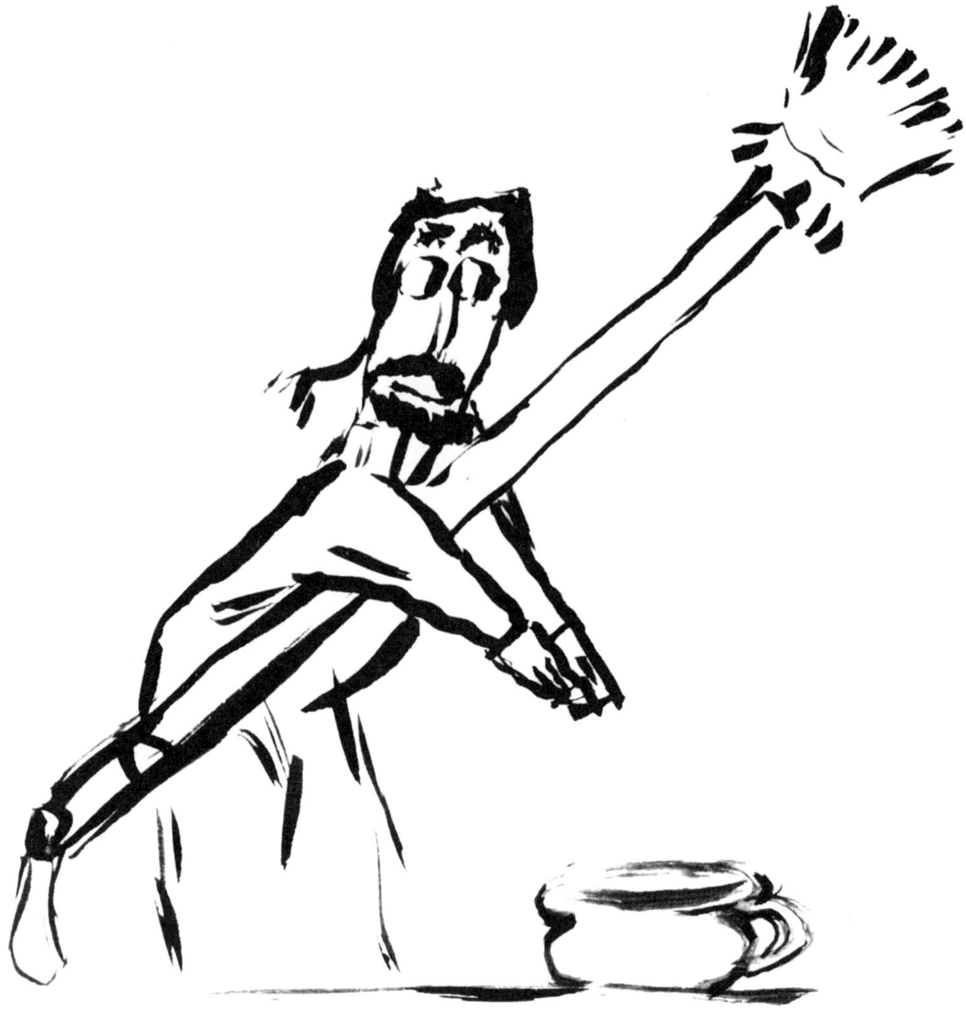

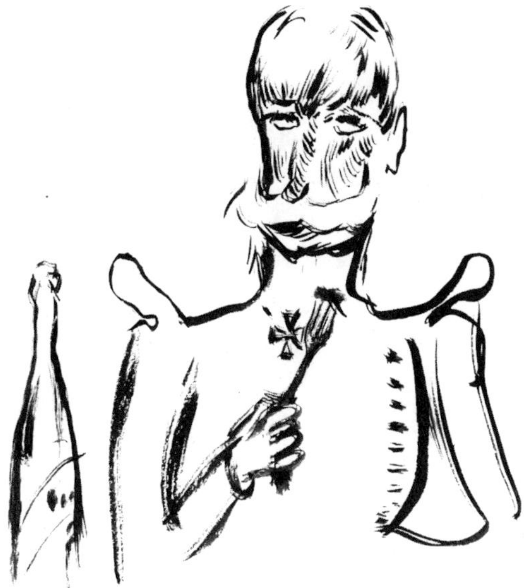

The Superkaiser

I was dining with my friend Baron von B and we were enjoying our third bottle of sparkling Moselle. At a nearby table a German general, very grand, haughty, monocled and redfaced from tight buttoning, was turning even redder as a result of heavy drinking. In front of him two cavalry officers, having made their bows and clicked their heels, stood rigidly to attention. I watched as the old warrior, without batting an eyelid, kept them standing motionless and humiliated for more than a minute, their elbows on a level with their chin, their buttocks indecently tense below the sky-blue hussars' jackets. After which he dismissed them with a curt gesture. I turned to my friend. 'Tell me,' I said, 'about the Kaiser.'

'The Emperor?' he replied wryly after a moment. 'Well, it's not very easy . . . however closely you know a man, especially of that calibre, you can never know him completely . . . but what the hell!' He removed the frosted bottle from the ice-bucket and refilled our glasses.

'You have to realise,' he continued, 'that the Founders of 1871 were upstarts. They left for the frontier Prussians and poor; they returned from Paris Germans and millionaires. Nothing brings out the worst instincts like a victory; it puffs us up and prevents us from thinking. It begets only brutes . . . .

'So they set about building Germany . . . we are not frugal as a nation, we enjoy eating noisily and drinking a lot, and we like building –
fortresses and cannons; harbours,
ships and cannons; roads,
canals and cannons . . . barracks,
factories, palaces

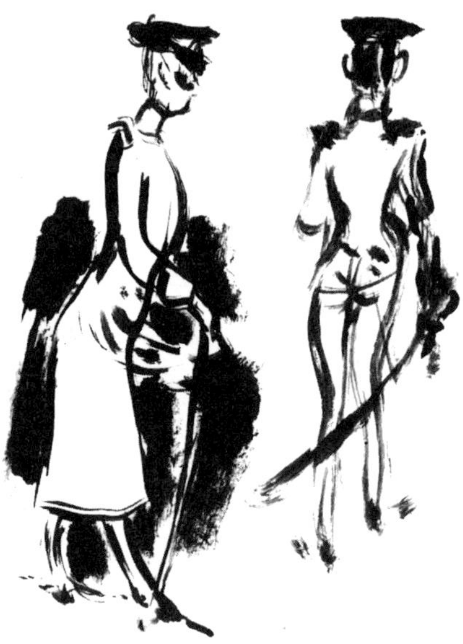

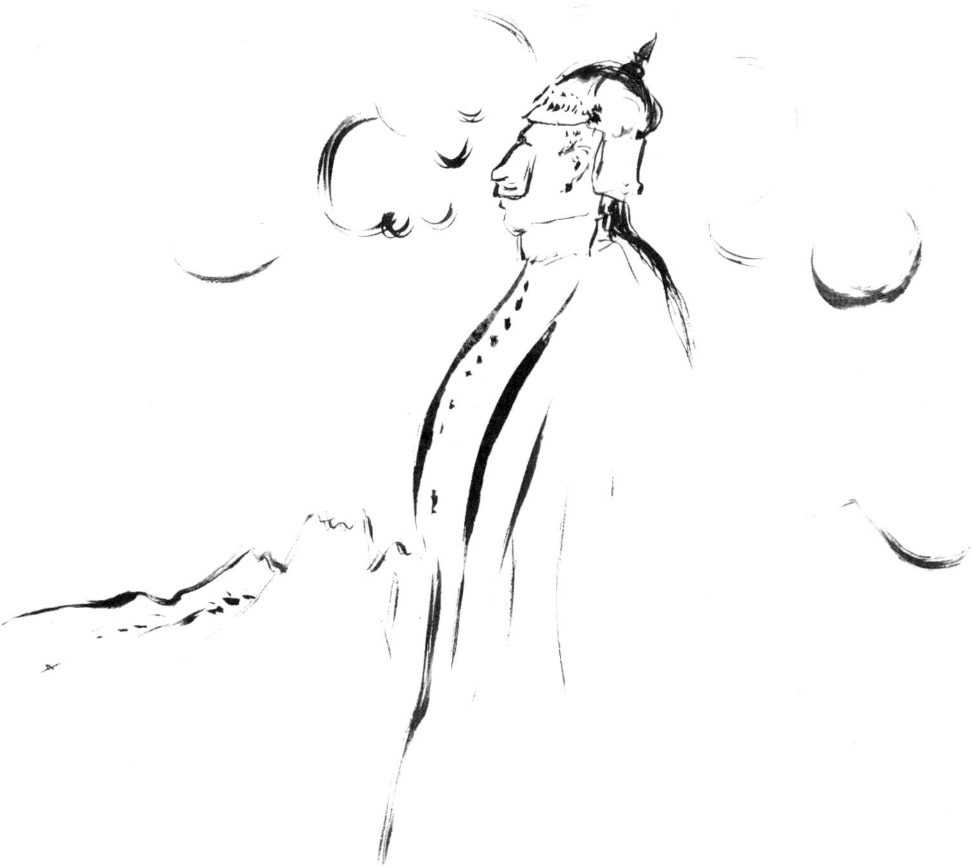

and still more cannons. Berlin was rebuilt, the whole of Germany was rebuilt, from end to end . . . towns in keeping with the capital. And we go on building bigger and bigger – colossal statues, giant universities, fortress-like railway stations, Babylonian post-offices, shops like cathedrals, Valhalla-type restaurants. It all dates from the *Gründerzeit*, the time of the Founders. And Wilhelm II also dates from those years of megalomania, from the excesses of those upstarts with their self-importance, bad manners, flashiness and tinpot grandeur. He was only a young man then, but you retain all your life the ideas with which your head was filled when you were twenty . . . .

'Now he sits ensconced on an imperial throne that he didn't win, heir to an epic victory in which he didn't lift a finger, prancing around on manoeuvres as if it was still continuing – not just a 'daddy's boy' but a 'grand-daddy's boy' as well . . . . There are two very distinct people in Wilhelm, who seem mutally exclusive: the man, who is charming and whom I like, and the Emperor, whom I detest.

'To listen to him in private, sprawled in an armchair, legs crossed, smoking his pipe and roaring with laughter, without a trace of arrogance or pompousness, you would never dream that this was the formidable despot and clumsy

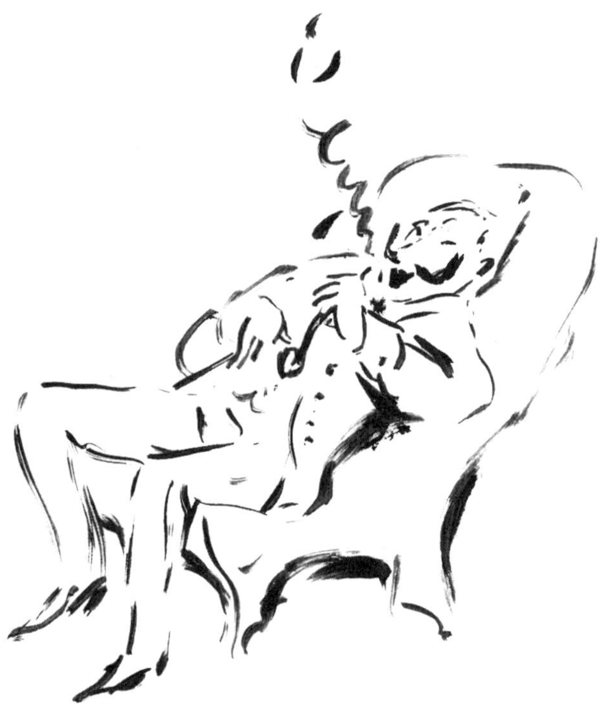

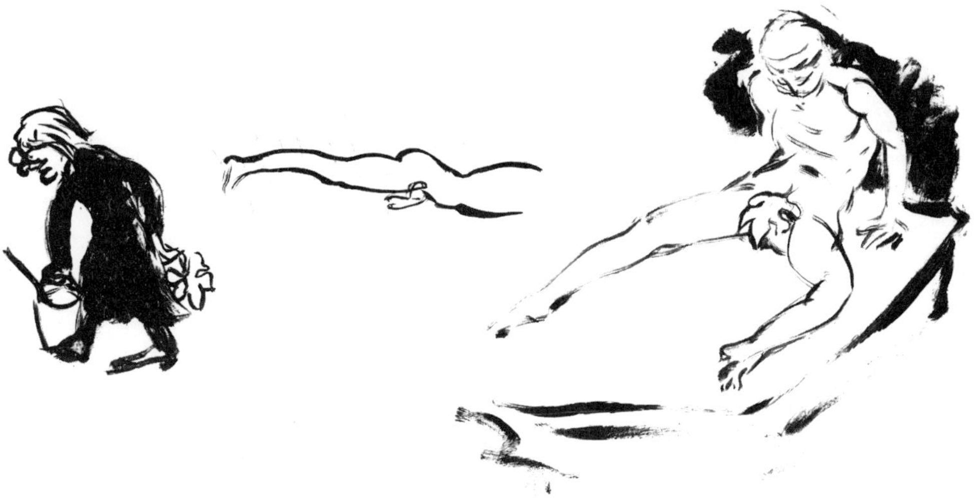

nonentity who keeps the
nerves of Europe on edge and
terrorises the world with his sabre-rattling!

'As for the Empress, she is totally lacking in that quality which is most necessary to her sex: charm. She is virtuous – indeed virtue incarnate, and therefore miserable, bad-tempered, biased and without a vestige of kindness. You will be amused to learn that she has taken upon herself the duty of censoring opera performances, conscientiously deleting the word "love" from all native productions and tolerating it only in works derived from the French. And another obsession which has made people laugh is her insistence, when visiting a museum, that all nudity in pictures and statues be covered or removed during her visit . . . .'

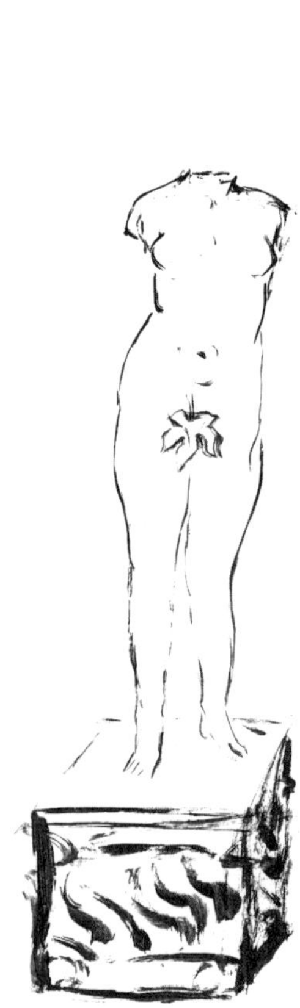

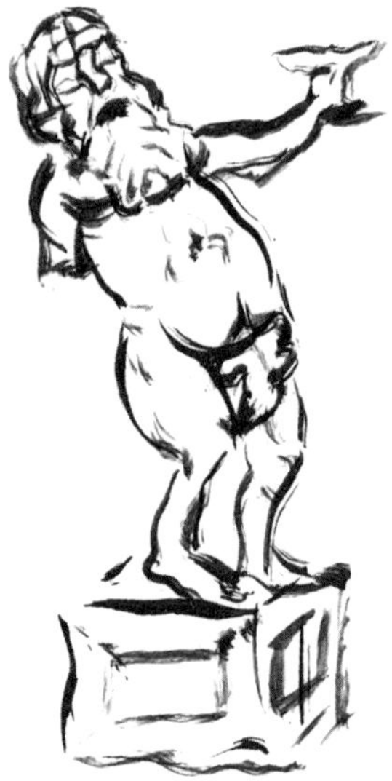

'Mind you,' added von B, 'The Kaiser has his foibles too. Would you believe that in a country where they are practically a religion, he loathes flowers? Yes, he absolutely detests them, whether in gardens or window-boxes, or even represented in works of art.'

'Why? Does he regard them as dangerous, like Socialists?'

'No, he just finds them ugly . . . as he finds statues by Rodin ugly, and the glorious flesh tints of Renoir . . . . He would like to see our lawns and parks adorned with masses of sabres, baskets full of shells, beds of bayonets and field-guns. Let me tell you a story . . . .

'In his will a very wealthy man left to the city of Berlin that monumental fountain in the Schlossplatz. I find it quite stylish, and the foundry-work is excellent – in fact

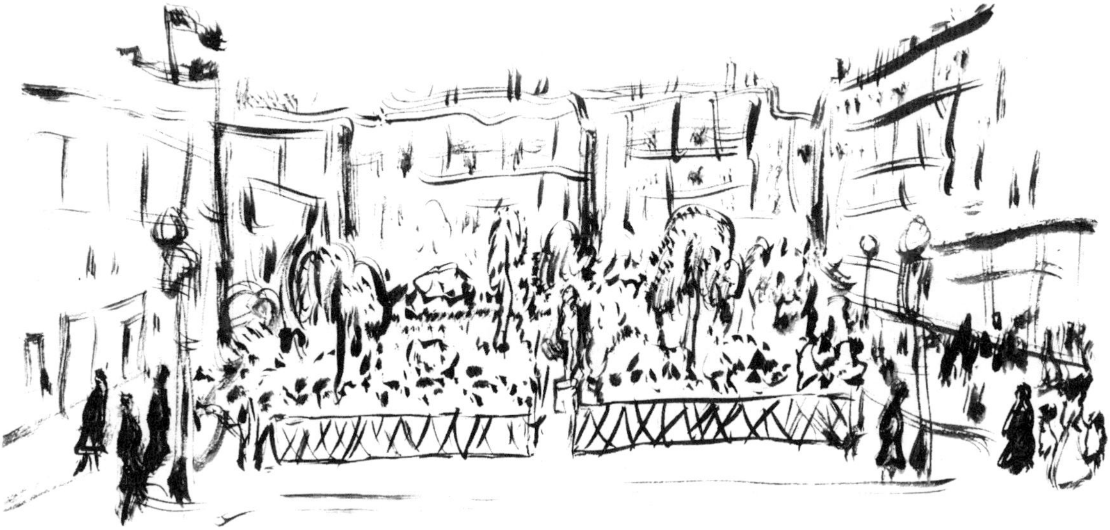

it's the best thing of its kind in Berlin.

The mayor invited the Emperor to the unveiling; but Wilhelm, who had tried to prevent the bequest being accepted by every possible legal and administrative ruse, refused the invitation point-blank, almost rudely. It was inconceivable that any monument should be erected in Berlin that was not his idea, designed by him, the model moulded with his own fair hands. It seemed an insult to his authority, almost treasonable. He was furious. We spoke about it together, for it was preying on his mind, and one evening he swore at me in French: "That bloody fountain! It's a Socialist conspiracy!" I tried to calm him down, but he cut me short. "*Parbleu*! I know what it is . . . you're a Socialist too. Everyone is nowadays. They'd better look out!"

'On the day of the unveiling the crowd was astonished to see the Kaiser appear, his face dark and menacing. He interrupted the speaker who was singing the praises of the benefactor, and harangued the crowd as follows:

'"An evil spirit broods over our city. Socialism is raising its head. I will not tolerate it! The barracks are filled with loyal troops and my faithful artillery. If the Socialists stir one step I shall not hesitate, for the good of the country, to mow them down. Let them be warned. I shall mow them down. I have had enough!" He glanced at the fountain, shrugged his shoulders and muttered, so that only those on the platform could hear: "As for this fountain, it's ridiculous, ridiculous . . . Pah!" And he stomped off as furiously as he had arrived. The odd thing is that the incident was hushed up, even in Germany. It was discussed, discreetly in whispers, but not a word escaped abroad. It's just that we Germans have a sort of national prudery – stupid really – which makes us throw a cloak over the Emperor's antics, like the sons of Noah covering their father's nakedness.'

Von B told me another extraordinary story about Wilhelm and his treatment of his mother on the very day of his accession, as recounted to him by Bismarck himself.

'Wilhelm's father, the Emperor Frederick, had for years kept a diary, the existence of which filled young Wilhelm with terror. Did they contain criticism of his conduct? Did they express dangerous sentiments? As his father lay dying Wilhelm's one thought was to secure possession of those papers. But the Empress, his mother, had already placed them in safe keeping and despite her son's closest surveillance had sent them to England, either to her own mother, Queen Victoria, or to her brother, the Prince of Wales.

'Hardly had he arisen from his father's deathbed than the new Emperor demanded the diary. His mother feigned ignorance, but he insisted, positively commanding her to obey him. She stuck to her story . . . . She knew nothing of the matter . . . . Wilhelm resorted to threats. The more she resisted, the more he blustered, for surely her obstinacy was a measure of the document's importance. Actually he couldn't bear the thought of anyone, however high-ranking, defying him at the very outset of the reign for which he had waited so long. Rage transformed the day-old Emperor into a raving lunatic. "Very well, ma'am", he bellowed, purple with fury, "you are under arrest! Close arrest, ma'am, until my orders are obeyed!"

'Bismarck arrived a couple of hours later from Potsdam to find the palace surrounded by squadrons of armed cavalry. The Emperor told him how he had dealt with his mother's disobedience. He was still very excited, glowing with his splendid idea. "And she needn't expect any pity from me, any weakening, Mr Chancellor, not until she does as she's told!"

'The Chancellor, looking back on it, wondered how he had managed not to burst out laughing in his sovereign's face . . . . But he knew he must preserve a respectful silence to mark his disapproval, and then suggest harsher, more effective measures. Why not cut off the Empress's supplies? Suspend her privileges? "I know Her Majesty," he observed. "She has her pride. Close arrest she can bear . . . accept as a sort of martyrdom. But money, Sire . . . money? Who can resist money?" The Emperor, having by now calmed down, accepted the advice. The arrest of the Empress was lifted. The troops returned to barracks . . . . And Wilhelm drew up plans for the funeral and court mourning.

'But how did the story end?' I enquired.

'The struggle between the Empress and her son lasted for months. It was at least six months before the Emperor got his manuscript and the Empress her money.... Oh, she was quite a girl!'

I asked von B an obvious question.

'Do you believe the Kaiser is thinking of war?'

'Not on your life,' he cried. 'Never! For all his uniforms, despite the sabre-rattling, Wilhelm is no warrior. He is a soldier, which is very different. But he's not even brave... like your Napoleon, who sweated with fear at the noise of gunfire.

'Those speeches of his, those antics and threats – just tricks of the trade. He throws Europe into a scare now and then simply to reassure the big arms manufacturers and keep the factories going full blast.... Another reason that prevents the Kaiser from declaring war is that he's scared of the result. True, our army is strong, the strongest in the world. But we only have parade-ground officers who do no work and think only of their pleasures: gambling, women, even men. They are totally depraved. And as for the High Command, it's second rate, quite ghastly, in the hands of courtier-generals, bloated with honours and wealth, who have climbed up through intrigue, dirty dealing and scandalous conduct.

'And ponder this appalling thought. In case of war, Wilhelm won't let anyone else command his armies. He plans for war as he plans for statues, pictures, operas and all the rest of it....'

Here von B assumed an expression of mock horror and exclaimed, 'And then, my friend, we should be beaten, even by Switzerland, I tell you! You don't believe me? I've been on manoeuvres and they're completely farcical. Absolutely hilarious! Even Switzerland...!'

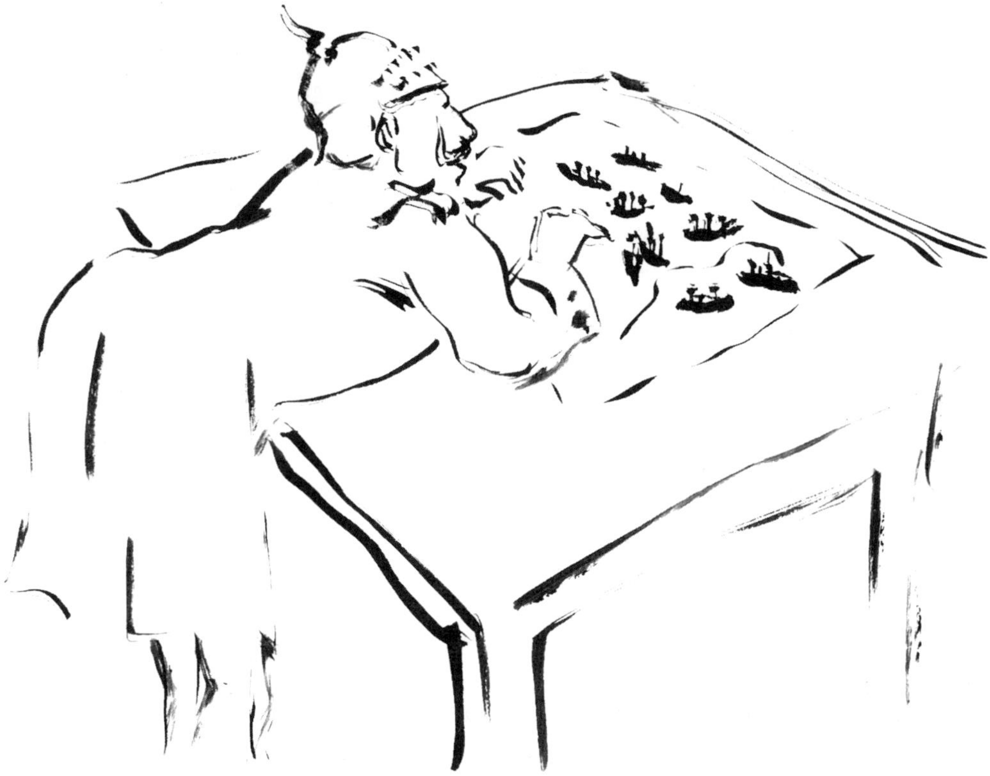

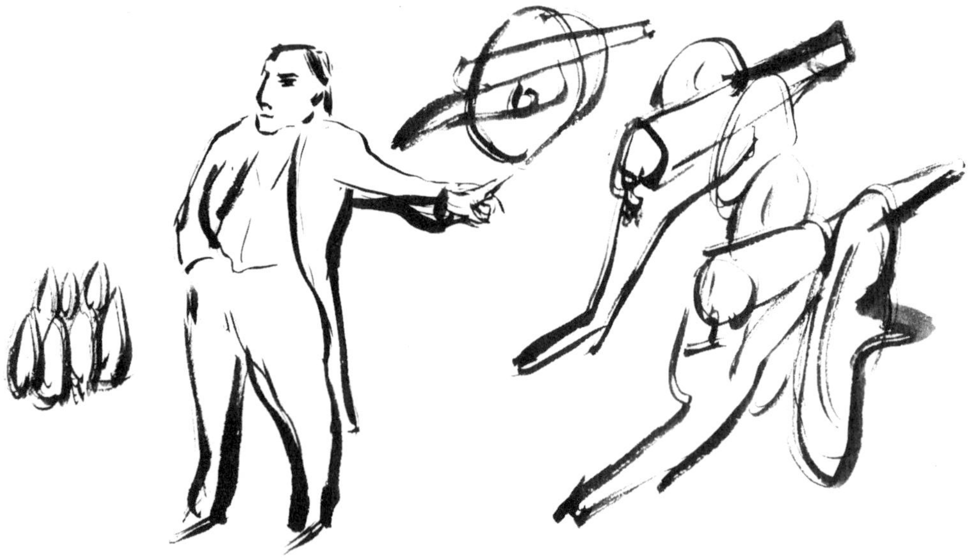

The piano factory

In Düsseldorf, the more an article costs the more loudly it proclaims that it is expensive and the prouder they are of it. This is typically American, and the same influence shows in the way they dress, the way the men go clean-shaven, even in the way they do business, where, according to Baron von B, they can be just as sharp and unexpectedly humorous about it. He told me of an occasion last year when he took a French friend on a tour round the factories of Herr Erhardt, the famous Düsseldorf gun-founder, the rival of Krupp.

'Aha!' cried Erhardt, shaking hands with his visitor, 'So, you've come to see my pianos?'

'*Comment?* Your pianos!'

'Yes indeed . . . Érard . . . your Érard. Only with me it's another kind of music, haha! Never mind,' chuckled Herr Erhardt. 'Forget it!'

The theatre of repopulation

We went to the theatre. They were giving *Monna Vanna*, the tragedy by Maeterlinck. This has been a tremendous success in Germany. The performances are conscientious but lifeless, the productions lavish but tasteless. The colours clash and the flashiness of the sets is blinding.

We had difficulty in getting seats. The house was packed, a sell-out. And the audience was ecstatic. During the interval von B remarked, 'What you are witnessing here, *mon cher*, is one of the strangest sights in Germany. And what is happening here in Düsseldorf is taking place simultaneously in forty other towns where *Monna Vanna* is playing tonight. Do you know the real reason for the unprecedented success of this tragedy? I will tell you. It is the most German thing in the world: in the second act Monna Vanna goes to Princevalle's tent "naked under her cloak". . . .'

'Well?' I inquired.

'But that's it! "Naked under her cloak". Just that! I don't say for a moment that my countrymen aren't moved by the supreme beauty of the play, by its marvellous, incomparable poetry. No indeed. Whatever people say, a German appreciates grandeur in a work of imagination. Furthermore he is tremendously fond of the theatre, especially French plays. Yes, but this one – well, it offers a bit more. Monna Vanna is "naked under her cloak". Kindly mark this. If suddenly, with a bold gesture she were to fling off her cloak – if she stood there in her radiant nudity against the red background of the tent and the wild animal skins on the bed – they would be terribly shocked, they would protest and the tension would be broken. But Monna Vanna is infinitely more naked than "without her

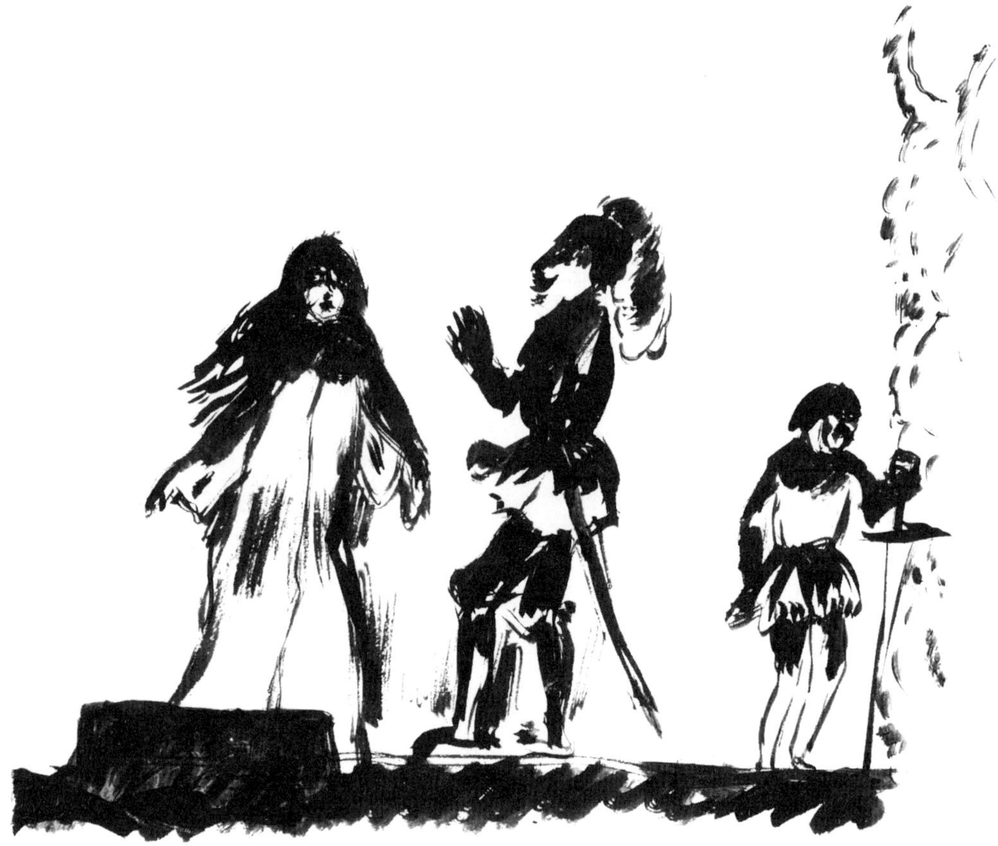

cloak". Did you see how tensely they stare, how their pupils are dilated as though by belladonna, how still they sit? Did you observe how some of the men had closed their eyes, as if to isolate that image, to caress it, to bring it to life? All the hidden passion, the suppressed desire at the thought that Monna Vanna was "naked under her cloak". Licit sensuality, permissible lechery – like dreaming, it increases tenfold the power of the imagination.

'And later tonight something stranger still will happen. No one in that audience will take dinner after the theatre. They will rush home, all hot and trembling, their minds filled with Monna Vanna "naked under her cloak"; and they will produce for the Fatherland a little German baby . . . . It is quite astonishing, *mon cher*, how one actress, who incidentally is not the least naked under her cloak, can in one evening increase the population of a large country like Germany. Perhaps one day the statisticians will reveal it all.'

And he added, 'I can't fathom, by the way, why in your country as in mine, there are so many earnest idiots who want to banish sensuality from the stage, from literature and art. Even what they call pornography should be respected and protected as a force, as a national asset, since it encourages the sexes to come together . . . .'

'So,' said I, 'you're all in favour of repopulation?'

'Me?' chuckled von B. 'I really couldn't give a damn, old boy!'

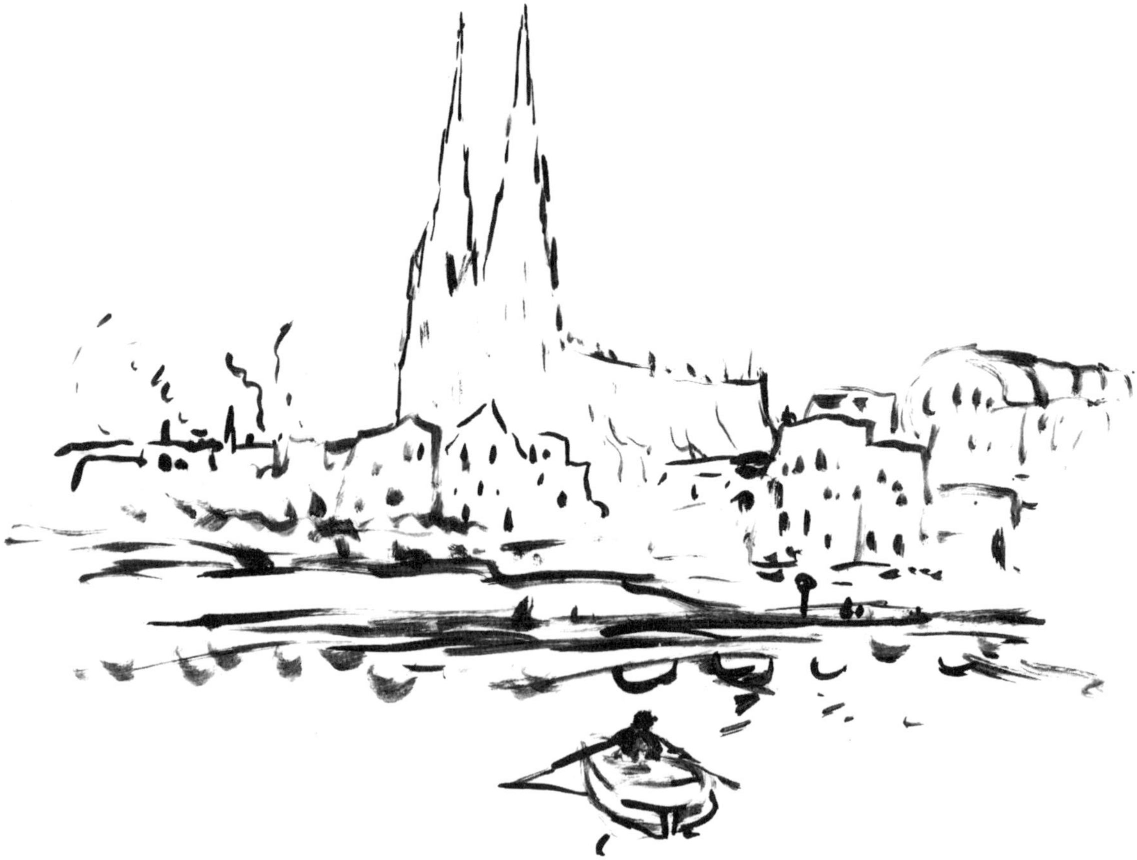

Cologne

The journey to Cologne was most
exhausting. There were roadworks
everywhere, for repairs, linking-up
or widening – ruts, potholes and piles of rubble. On three
occasions I had to enlist the aid of horses – what

humiliation! – to rescue The 628-E8 when stuck in the mire. The main roads into villages and towns were always closed so that we had to go round by wet, rough, muddy tracks through the fields, and it was a wonder the car didn't finish as a write-off. On rebuilt stretches the authorities had with devilish cunning left large square cobblestones lying about, and to avoid them we had to execute perilous manoeuvres comparable to a sword-dance. Faced with these obstacles, Brossette's nationalism reasserted itself, and he reverted to mumbling, 'Rotten country!', as a mild substitute for a string of imprecations.

Certainly Brossette's place behind the wheel was no sinecure; his wrists were worn out and he was dripping with sweat. To add to our woes von B, who, for the sake of friendship (the devil take his friendship!), was accompanying us in his Mercedes, ran out of petrol. This kept us hanging round in the open countryside for about two hours, and all for nothing, because when Brossette finally emerged from under the Mercedes, he announced that the whole engine would have to be stripped down, and possibly the body as well. What could we do? Abandon our uninvited companion out there on the road? It was tempting, but alas impossible. Eventually we had to tow the Mercedes the twenty kilometres or so to Cologne.

By the time we drove into Cologne, headlights on, it was dark. We stopped in front of the Cathedral Hotel, overshadowed by what is the most colossal, most ugly cathedral in the world . . . .

I slept very badly, tossing and turning, suffering nightmares because of the proximity of that maddening cathedral. Time itself, which wears everything away, seems to have had no effect on that unrelenting stone. Neither rain nor sun nor frost have managed to soften its spiky angles and harsh lines. As I slept, its weight stifled and crushed

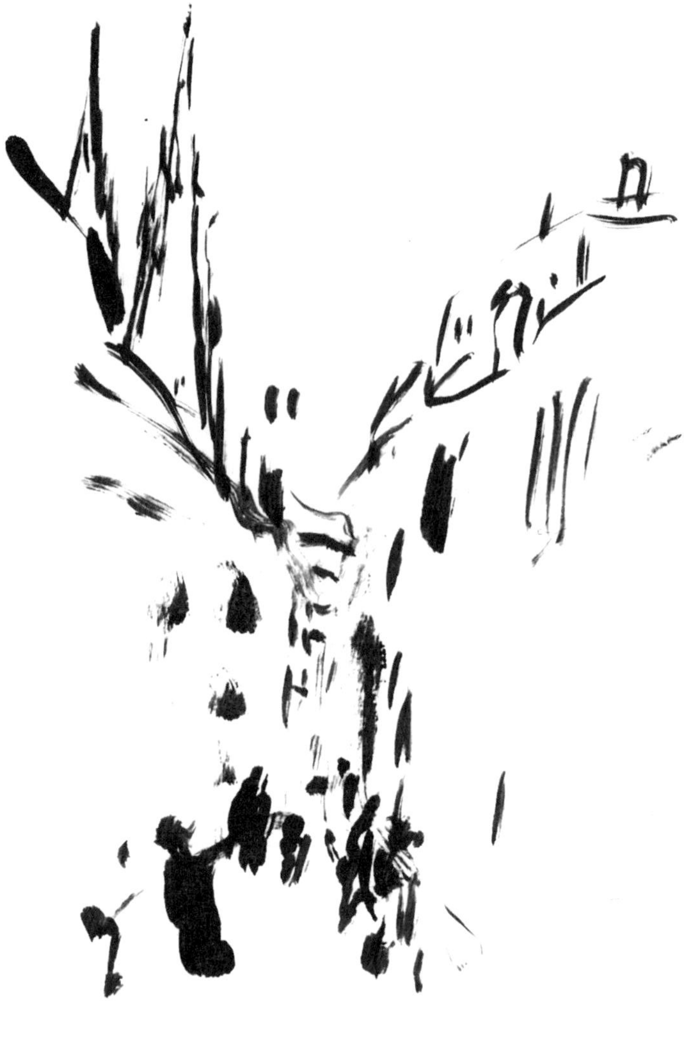

me, and from the ground to the topmost pinnacle, thousands of hideously probing knives cut deep into my body like instruments of torture. I awoke with a start, gasping, in a cold sweat.

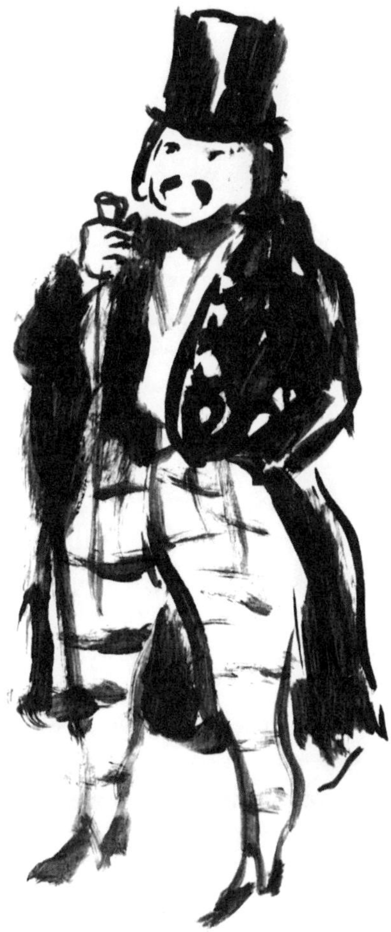

Balzac

Among the many French books
in a Cologne shop window I spotted the *Letters*
of Balzac, in the octavo edition. I bought it and returned to

the hotel, knowing immediately that my stroll had been worthwhile. As I hurried back, it began to rain, a fine drizzle that cast a funereal gloom over the city.

That afternoon I encouraged my companions to go out and shut myself in my room with my acquisition.

I adore Balzac – not only as the creator of that wonderful cast of characters in *La Comédie humaine*, but also as an extraordinary man, a human prodigy.

His life – or what is known of it – resembled his works: it was vast, tumultuous, a torrent carrying all before it. Unfortunately we know little of it.

He was short, squat, dumpy, overweight and very ugly . . . . But the moment he started speaking, the magic worked. His words had such authority, such charm, that one forgot his ungainly appearance. The intelligence in his eyes gave his face beauty. He was conscious of his power to fascinate, as he was conscious of his genius. Balzac created love as he created a book. Women found him irresistible.

I have been told that when talking about women Balzac would puff himself up like a turkey-cock. But he was never one to kiss and tell; despite his sometimes comical self-conceit, he was infinitely discreet. This discretion, rare in a man of letters, we find irritating, because it hides him from us even more. He whose fame throughout Europe had made his features familiar everywhere had the gift of making himself invisible whenever he wished . . . .

He would mislead the inquisitive, put spies off the scent and make use of his friends, who never suspected the role they were being called on to play. One day he disappeared from Paris. Where was he? Had he shut himself in to work? Was he travelling to collect material for a book? Was it a love affair or a business trip?

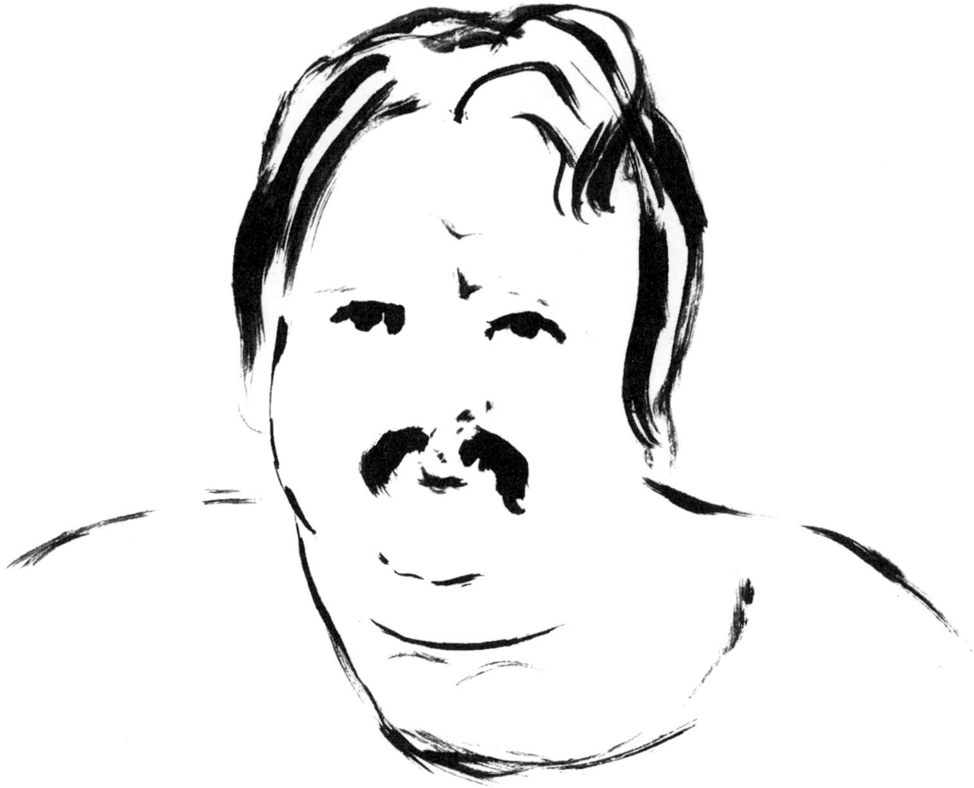

His absence lasted a year, two years.

Then suddenly, one fine evening, with no prior word to his household, he reappeared. Once again he was seen at the Opéra, with his blue dress suit and his cane, the knob of which – so he claimed – was carved in gold melted down from his lady-friends' bracelets. He might have been resuming conversations interrupted the day before and he seemed to be conversant with all the current gossip. Concerning his absence, not a word.

Everything about him was vast, his virtues and vices. He felt everything, desired everything, accomplished everything that is human . . . . His life was a permanent furnace of creativity, a perpetual longing, a terrible struggle.

Thoughts, feelings, rumbled away inside him like lava in an active volcano. With an ease that is bewildering, he could keep four books going at once, together with controversial newspaper articles, business matters, love affairs, lawsuits, travels, debts, collections, social engagements, a huge correspondence, and ill-health. Amid all this there was scarcely a sign of slackening, discouragement, self-doubt; no let-up. That indefatigable spirit sustained the overworked body, lifting it when it faltered. Having re-created the world, Balzac did not rest on the seventh day. Balzac courted Mme Hanska, a beautiful young Russian countess married to an older man, by correspondence for fifteen years, during which time they met on only four occasions. She harboured romantic dreams of the renowned writer and of Paris. Disregarding the inconvenience of an existing husband, they agreed to marry. But as a result of the 1848 Revolution he was financially ruined, while she was wealthy. Eventually he set off for Russia. No matter what, he would come back with a wife . . . and a fortune. Meeting Victor Hugo on the day before his departure, he said:

'Yes, I'm off to Russia . . . . Business. I shall come back with ten million francs.'

He was away for twenty months, during which time he changed enormously. He became overbearing and despotic . . . and he was seriously ill. Mme Hanska's circle turned her against the marriage. Even the Tsar, it is said, applied his veto. Yet presumably Balzac's eloquence, or perhaps pity on her part, finally prevailed. One evening in May 1850, Balzac returned to Paris, married. Married and practically dying . . . .

Around midnight he and his wife, exhausted after their journey, alighted outside No. 12 Avenue Fortunée. Before leaving Russia, he had written at length to his mother asking her to have the house in order, festively decorated. He wanted everything neat and tidy, flowers everywhere, a fine dinner ready. And he begged her, when all this was done, to go home, as he would prefer to introduce her new daughter-in-law formally the next day. His mother carried out her son's instructions and left everything in the hands of a manservant, hired for the occasion.

They arrive. The house is lit up, they can see the flowers inside. They ring the bell. No answer. They ring again. Nothing. A large lantern illuminates the double row of steps to the front door . . . but all is silent. Balzac is alarmed. He calls, shouts, hammers on the wrought-iron gate. Still nothing. Some late passers-by, thinking there has been an accident or a crime, offer to help. They add their knocking and their shouts to his . . . in vain. Meanwhile the cabbie has unloaded their luggage on to the pavement. Mme de Balzac feels cold, wraps her cloak more tightly about her, walks up and down, stamping her feet impatiently. Balzac, fuming, explains:

'This is incredible. I am M. de Balzac. This is my house . . . . I'm just back from abroad. We're expected . . . . I just don't understand!'

Someone volunteers to fetch a locksmith from a neighbouring street. While waiting, they continue hammering and shouting, to no effect. The little crowd grows. Mme de Balzac sits down on a trunk, head in hands.

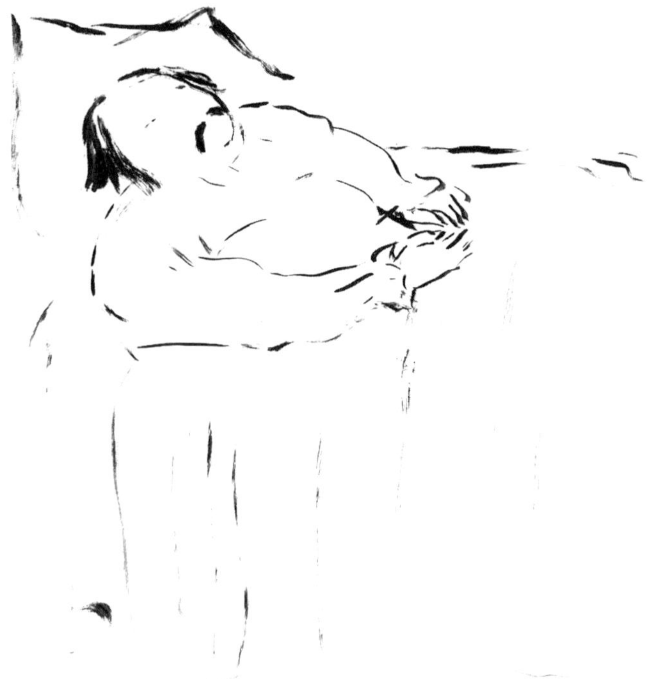

At last the locksmith arrives and forces open the gate. Followed by some of his newly found friends, eager to protect him from who knows what, Balzac hurries across the little yard and into his house.

An extraordinary sight greets him. The manservant has suddenly gone mad. He has plundered the dinner, scattering and smashing the crockery. Furniture has been overturned, flowers are strewn on the parquet floor and a broken bottle has leaked its frothy contents on to the carpet. Meanwhile the unfortunate footman is capering about – literally like a madman. He is caught, secured and locked up, submitting without a struggle, giggling instead of defending himself. Calm restored, Balzac thanks his gallant helpers, apologises, sees them out, has the luggage brought in and goes to bed. He is choking. He has a high fever. Slumped in a corner of the room, his wife is too exhausted even to remove her travelling cloak and weeps uncontrollably.

This little adventure was to have a profound effect on her. She saw it as the worst possible omen. Yet it was no longer a question of augury, but of facing painful reality. The stark, inexorable fact was that they had returned married – and enemies.

Of that great love affair, which fifteen years' absence had raised to giddy heights, and which a few months of life together had sufficed to destroy, there now remained nothing. And it might be true to say that their real separation dated from that moment when, bound to each other, they first entered that house.

Balzac was nearly always ill in bed. A circle of iron tightened increasingly around his chest. He spent his nights gasping in front of an open window, trying vainly to snatch a breath of air. His legs were swollen, oozing; the oedema was spreading to his abdomen, to his chest. He never complained, never gave up hope. As confidently as he had looked forward to the recovery of his fortunes, he awaited his recovery, so that he could get back to work, with an energy, a youthfulness, an immense creative drive which sustained him in his agony. While his body putrefied, his brain remained healthy, intact. He never ceased making plans, projects for books, synopses, outlines of plays, accumulating material for future publications. He had lost none of his marvellous creativity. Every day he would ask his physician, the faithful Dr Nacquart, 'Do you think I shall be able to get back to work tomorrow? Hurry up, there's so much to do . . . .'

(Eugène Honoré de Balzac died on 18 August 1850.)

Mainz

In Mainz, my friend von B took me to dine with a rich industrialist friend. His house was prettily arranged, rather like an English home, where solid comfort complements the demands of everyday life. The furniture, some of it too massive, some too flimsy, was not always sufficiently conventional and well designed for my taste, but at least it did not display the most hideous aspects of Art Nouveau. I was delighted to see nothing but French paintings on the walls, chosen with a bold but unerring eye; some lovely landscapes by Claude Monet, powerful still-lifes by Cézanne, splendid Renoir nudes. The dining-room had some exquisite panels by Vuillard. And in the study, decorations by Pierre Bonnard, sober, substantial, harmonious, with his sharp, incisive taste for capturing movement, that quality of subject and richness of colour that are his alone.

Elsewhere, van Goghs, Vallottons, extraordinarily expressive and light, fluid Roussels, worthy of Corot or Poussin. A large Courbet – a rocky landscape in the Jura – occupied a place of honour in the drawing-room. A whole suite of Lautrec pastels, some of them very free; watercolours, drawings by Guys and by Forain added a gay touch to the brightly lit staircase and landing. There was an abundance of sculpture, too, notably bronzes by Rodin and delightful wood-carvings by Maillol. . . .

My cultured hostess, too, was proud of her art collection and admired Vallotton, who, as she pointed out, was 'not yet appreciated in France' . . . . What a contrast to certain empty *poseuses* in Paris. Such stupid whims are unknown to German women. What I like especially in Germany, what I consider most precious

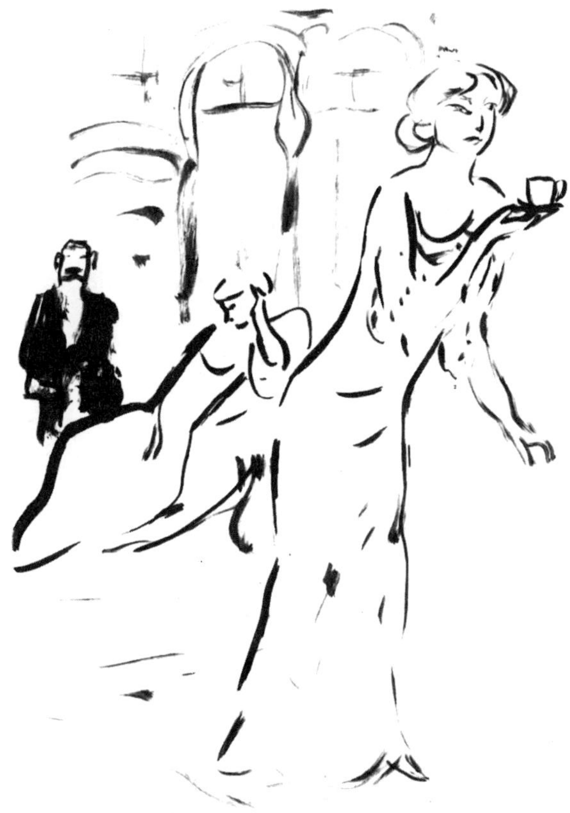

of all feminine accomplishments, is that even their most well informed ladies manage to remain womanly, never pedantic. They do not regard their duties as wife, mother or hostess as humiliating, and do not view them with embarrassment, boredom or distaste; they fit them in perfectly well with their intellectual pursuits.

Alsace

Today Strasbourg is a magnificent town, brand-new, with broad streets, fine white houses and gay window-boxes; we have nothing like it in France.

I had a long talk with a most intelligent native of Alsace who said, 'Strasbourg is completely Germanised. A few middle-class families still hold out, but their resistance consists merely of sitting around of an evening and mulling over old times, in French. . . . The very few Alsatians who remain are lost amid the flood of Germans who poured in after the annexation. They are not the cream of Germany; and our public servants – all German – are not the cream of the civil service either. Many left bad records behind. Instead of being sent to jail, they were sent to Alsace. . . .'

When I mentioned the tremendous redevelopment of the town, he murmured vaguely, 'Mm, yes, it's mostly window-dressing, though. Underneath there's a good deal of misery . . . or at any rate discomfort. The economic crisis which has struck the German industrial centres has affected us as well. We are crushed by taxation. Life is horribly expensive, forty-five per cent more than before. Morally and politically, we remain under German rule just as we were under French: docile, passive and discontented. . . .'

'So, all in all, how do you feel?' I asked.

He replied simply, 'Heavens above! One goes on living anyway. If one can't be oneself – Turkish, Laplander, Croat – it's all the same.'

'And Lorraine?'

'Ah, that's another story. Lorraine has remained French to the very depths of her soul. Smiles, threats, nothing affects that obstinate old feeling . . . like hope!'

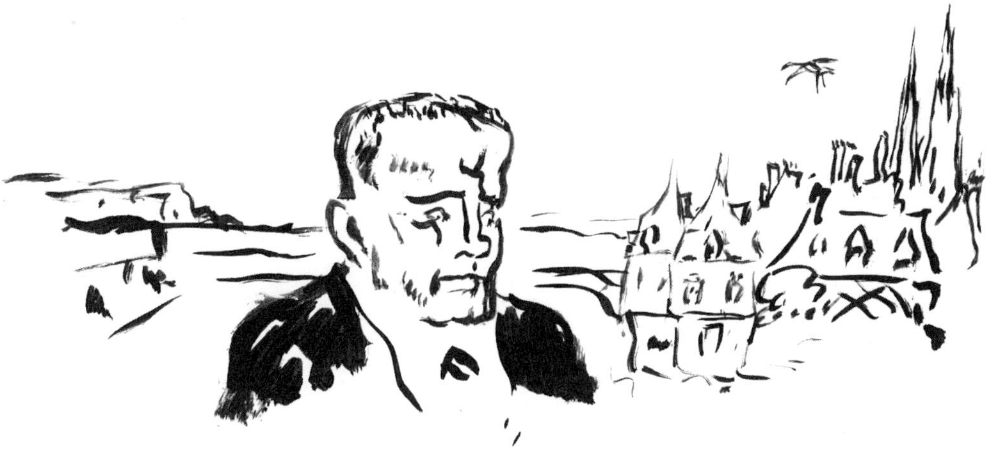

We spent five days touring through Alsace, its barley fields, its vineyards, its lovely pinewoods, its gently rolling hills, the colours of old velvet. The soft light and pale moving skies recalled the infinite transparencies of Holland. Nature, happily unaware of the frontiers which separate mankind, the boundaries which shift back and forth from time to time as our stupid squabbles dictate, is just the same as ever. . . .

Eventually we arrived, late in the evening, at the frontier, a place called Grand-Fontaine, a pretty village with neat little chalets strung out along the sides of a green field in the Vosges. It was half-past eight and we had the crazy notion of driving on to Baccarat for the night. The German customs man saw to the formalities. Despite the late hour he made no objection to refunding our deposit.

'As a matter of fact,' he said, 'I happen to have it in French money, I expect you'd rather have it that way.'

The customs post was clean and tidy, the men very spit-and-polish in their green tunics. They wished us *bon voyage.*

At Raon-la-Plaine, the French customs, we were treated like dogs. A stinking hole, a filthy sewer, that was our frontier for you. The houses seemed miserable and sordid, discordant sounds issued from a café.

A customs official dashed out in front of the car, brandishing a lantern. He was short and skinny, with his cap jammed sideways on his head, a blue tie twisted into a string, and his tunic, unbuttoned, smeared with grease.

'What have you got in those cases and packages? Anyhow, it's too late tonight. We're shut!'

I entered the office to complain to the head man. The room was all upside-down, the floor slimy with dirt. There was no head man, though one individual was asleep on a bench, his head on a sack. He grunted and swore as the door opened.

In the street, people from the café surrounded the car and were glaring at us in a hostile manner – puny, sallow creatures, with churlish mouths and shifty eyes.

I decided to return to Grand-Fontaine for the night.

Next morning we had to pass through customs. The inspector made it as ignominious as he could. He rummaged through our belongings, broke one of the bottles in a dressing-case, made an inventory, piece by piece, of every article in the tool-kit, and even took a Kodak out of its case to see what was hidden underneath. This continued for an hour. I wrote out a complaint. But where would a complaint go to?

Finally he allowed us to leave – furious at having found nothing suspicious, but delighted to have caused us trouble.

As we passed the last house of that disgusting village, someone threw a stone which broke one of our windows. I got off with a slightly scratched cheek.

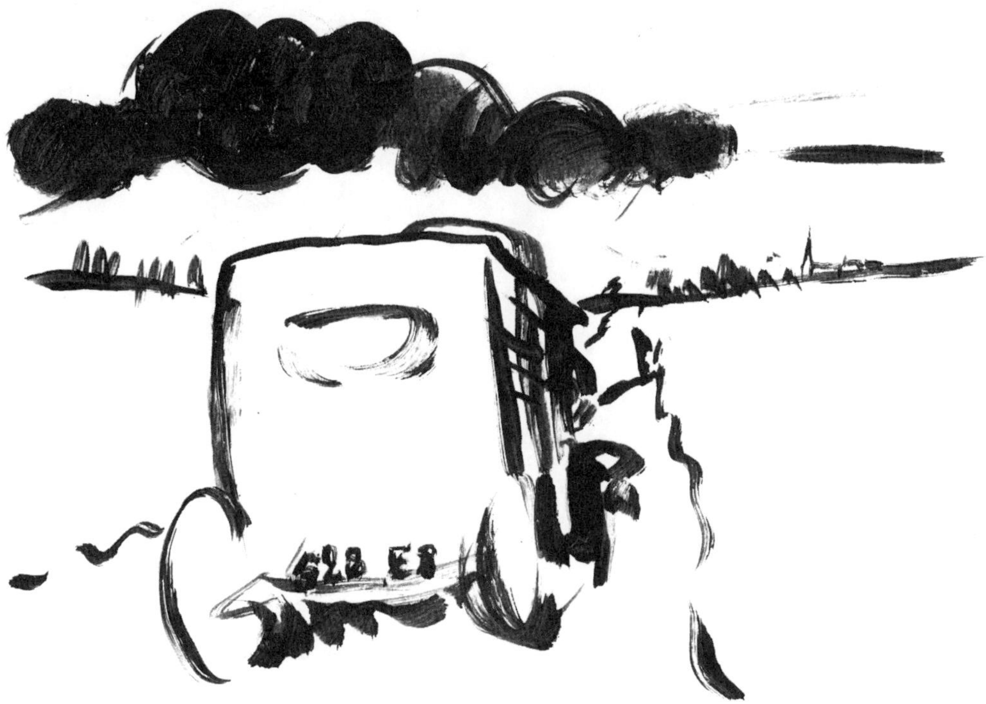

'Well, now,' I remarked, 'we're back in France, and no mistake!'

'Rotten place,' grumbled Brossette.

I think he was referring only to Raon-la-Plaine.

Paris, Corme Illes-en-Vexin, 1905–1907

The sketches

Details of sketches with page numbers

Original title page from the 1908 Fasquelle edition of *La 628-E8* 2
Cat approx 8.5 × 2cm (3$\frac{3}{8}$ × $\frac{3}{4}$in) 11
Departure 16.4 × 19.5cm (6$\frac{1}{2}$ × 7$\frac{3}{4}$in) 13
The tourist 22 × 18cm (8$\frac{3}{4}$ × 7$\frac{1}{8}$in) 15
The 628-E8 11 × 15.8cm (4$\frac{3}{8}$ × 6$\frac{1}{4}$in) 17
The canals of Holland 18 × 23cm (7$\frac{1}{8}$ × 9$\frac{1}{8}$in) 19
Dutch tulips 15.2 × 19.9cm (6 × 7$\frac{7}{8}$in) 20
Negress 17 × 14.5cm (6$\frac{3}{4}$ × 5$\frac{3}{4}$in) 22
Brossette 12 × 14.5cm (4$\frac{3}{4}$ × 5$\frac{3}{4}$in) 26
Brossette and the chambermaid 14.5 × 11.3cm (5$\frac{3}{4}$ × 4$\frac{1}{2}$in) 30
Gendarmes at La Capelle 23 × 18cm (9$\frac{1}{8}$ × 7$\frac{1}{8}$in) 33
The Customs lady at Elten 15.8 × 11.7cm (6$\frac{1}{4}$ × 4$\frac{5}{8}$in) 35
Customs inspection 16.4 × 13.2cm (6$\frac{1}{2}$ × 5$\frac{1}{4}$in) 35
The River Oise 18 × 30.6cm (7$\frac{1}{8}$ × 12$\frac{1}{8}$in) 37
Academicians 15.2 × 16.1cm (6 × 6$\frac{3}{8}$in) 38
Historians 15.2 × 16.4cm (6 × 6$\frac{1}{2}$in) 39
Defrauding the revenue 8.2 × 8.2cm (3$\frac{1}{4}$ × 3$\frac{1}{4}$in) 40
Politicians 12.6 × 8.5cm (5 × 3$\frac{3}{8}$in) 41
The River Meuse 18 × 24.3in (7$\frac{1}{8}$ × 9$\frac{5}{8}$in) 42
Breakdown 15.8 × 17.3cm (6$\frac{1}{4}$ × 6$\frac{7}{8}$in) 45
Full speed ahead 8.8 × 27.4cm (3$\frac{1}{2}$ × 10$\frac{7}{8}$in) 47
The paving stones of Belgium 11.3 × 22cm (4$\frac{1}{2}$ × 8$\frac{3}{4}$in) 48
Mediaeval Brussels 18 × 23cm (7$\frac{1}{8}$ × 9$\frac{1}{8}$in) 49
Lamplit encounter 17.5 × 9.9cm (6$\frac{7}{8}$ × 3$\frac{7}{8}$) 50
'The King's in on it' 13.5 × 5.6cm 5$\frac{3}{8}$ × 2$\frac{1}{4}$in) 51
Mother and young daughters 23 × 18cm (9$\frac{1}{8}$ × 7$\frac{1}{8}$in) 53
Mme B 14.8 × 9.5cm (5$\frac{7}{8}$ × 3$\frac{3}{4}$in) 55
Extreme unction 10.7 × 14.2cm (4$\frac{1}{4}$ × 5$\frac{5}{8}$in) 57
The striker's march 13.2 × 23cm (5$\frac{1}{4}$ × 9$\frac{1}{8}$in) 58
Riots in Ghent 17.3 × 20.8cm (6$\frac{7}{8}$ × 8$\frac{1}{4}$in) 60
Henri Houssaye surveying the battlefield of Waterloo 19.9 × 19.5cm (7$\frac{7}{8}$ × 7$\frac{3}{4}$in) (Houssaye wrote a treatise on the Battle of Waterloo) 61
The Flemish Giant 8.2 × 13.5cm (3$\frac{1}{4}$ × 5$\frac{3}{8}$in) 62
The giant rabbit and chickens 9.8 × 17cm (3$\frac{7}{8}$ × 6$\frac{3}{4}$in) 63
Flemish chickens 15.8 × 14.2cm (6$\frac{1}{4}$ × 5$\frac{5}{8}$in) 64
King Léopold and Mlle Cléo 16.4 × 13.8cm (6$\frac{1}{2}$ × 5$\frac{1}{2}$in) 67
Approaching Antwerp 20.2 × 18.9cm (8 × 7$\frac{1}{2}$in) 68
Brossette's wolfskin coat 12 × 15.8cm (4$\frac{3}{4}$ × 6$\frac{1}{4}$in) 69
The sailing boat 18 × 23cm (7$\frac{1}{8}$ × 9$\frac{1}{8}$in) 71
The docks of Antwerp 17.3 × 23cm (6$\frac{7}{8}$ × 9$\frac{1}{8}$in) 72
The quayside 17.7 × 23cm (7 × 9$\frac{1}{8}$) 72
The port 18 × 30.6cm (7$\frac{1}{8}$ × 12$\frac{1}{8}$in) 73
Two negro minstrels 23 × 17.3cm (9$\frac{1}{8}$ × 6$\frac{7}{8}$in) 74
The missionary 13.5 × 15cm (5$\frac{3}{8}$ × 6in) 75
The old jew from Russia 12 × 9.8cm (4$\frac{3}{4}$ × 3$\frac{7}{8}$in) 78
Pogrom 19.9 × 30.3cm (7$\frac{7}{8}$ × 12in) 80
Prostitutes 17 × 16.1cm (6$\frac{3}{4}$ × 6$\frac{3}{8}$in) 82
Sailors 19.2 × 10.1cm (7$\frac{5}{8}$ × 4in) 83
The girl from Kotonu 17 × 21.8cm (6$\frac{3}{4}$ × 8$\frac{5}{8}$in) 84
The longed-for horizon 18 × 29.3cm (7$\frac{1}{8}$ × 11$\frac{5}{8}$in) 86
Bolting Horse 11.7 × 18.6cm (4$\frac{5}{8}$ × 7$\frac{3}{8}$in) 87
The unforeseen obstacle 12.9 × 18.6cm (5$\frac{1}{8}$ × 7$\frac{3}{4}$in) 88
Gorinchem 15 × 18.9cm (6 × 7$\frac{1}{2}$in) 90
Monet's floating Japanese prints 23 × 17.7cm (9$\frac{1}{8}$ × 7in) 93
Canals of Amsterdam 12.3 × 15.2cm (4$\frac{7}{8}$ × 6in) 95
Amsterdam 18 × 12.4cm (7$\frac{1}{8}$ × 4$\frac{7}{8}$in) 96
The lost slipper 23 × 19.5cm (9$\frac{1}{8}$ × 7$\frac{3}{4}$in) 99
Boer farmer 9.8 × 9.8cm (3$\frac{7}{8}$ × 3$\frac{7}{8}$in) 100
Boer museum attendant 10.4 × 11cm (4$\frac{1}{8}$ × 4$\frac{3}{8}$in) 101
The open road (hitherto unpublished) 19.5 × 19.9cm (7$\frac{3}{4}$ × 7$\frac{7}{8}$in) 102
The platter of plover's eggs 12.9 × 18.6cm (5$\frac{1}{8}$ × 7$\frac{3}{8}$in) 104
The rising chemise 23.4 × 18cm (9$\frac{1}{4}$ × 7$\frac{1}{8}$in) 107
Life on the roads 19.9 × 30.3cm (7$\frac{7}{8}$ × 12in) 110
'Man's noblest conquest' 16.7 × 12.9cm (6$\frac{5}{8}$ × 5$\frac{1}{8}$in) 111
The frightened horse 12.6 × 10.1cm (5 × 4in) 112
Horse and cart 16.7 × 15cm (6$\frac{5}{8}$ × 6$\frac{1}{8}$in) 113
Cows – a rear view 12.6 × 13.8cm (5 × 5$\frac{1}{2}$in) 114
The goat 23 × 19.5cm (9$\frac{1}{8}$ × 7$\frac{3}{4}$in) 115
The cow 15.8 × 11cm (6$\frac{1}{4}$ × 4$\frac{3}{8}$in) 115
Cats on roof-top 23.4 × 19.9cm (9$\frac{1}{4}$ × 7$\frac{5}{8}$in) 116
Cat in contemplation 9.1 × 5.6cm (3$\frac{5}{8}$ × 2$\frac{1}{4}$in) 117
The pig 4.7 × 8.2cm (1$\frac{7}{8}$ × 3$\frac{1}{4}$in) 118
The donkey and the mule 10.1 × 16.7cm (4 × 6$\frac{5}{8}$in) 119
The master and his dog 17 × 15.2cm (6$\frac{3}{4}$ × 6in) 120
Flustered hen 14.5 × 8.2cm (5$\frac{3}{4}$ × 3$\frac{1}{4}$in) 121
Hens in flight 15.8 × 15.2cm (6$\frac{1}{4}$ × 6in) 122
Ducks 20.8 × 19.9cm (8$\frac{1}{4}$ × 7$\frac{7}{8}$in) 123
Geese 15.8 × 12.3cm (6$\frac{1}{4}$ × 4$\frac{7}{8}$in) 124
The rabbits of Germany 8.2 × 18.9cm (3$\frac{1}{4}$ × 7$\frac{1}{2}$in) 125
Disappearing rabbits 6 × 18.9cm (2$\frac{3}{8}$ × 7$\frac{1}{2}$in) 126
The road at night 23 × 19.5cm (9$\frac{1}{8}$ × 7$\frac{3}{4}$in) 127
'Martians' 23 × 19.9cm (9$\frac{1}{8}$ × 7$\frac{5}{8}$in) 129
The cyclist 11.7 × 10.7cm (4$\frac{5}{8}$ × 4$\frac{1}{4}$in) 131
Flattened 19.5 × 18cm (7$\frac{3}{4}$ × 7$\frac{1}{8}$in) 132
The impatient 628-E8 27.8 × 18cm (11 × 7$\frac{1}{8}$in) 135
The ferry crossing at Emmerich 18 × 23cm (7$\frac{1}{8}$ × 9$\frac{1}{8}$in) 137
An accident 15.8 × 13.8cm (6$\frac{1}{4}$ × 5$\frac{1}{2}$in) 139
'Intimate quarters' 15.2 × 11cm (6 × 4$\frac{3}{8}$in) 142
The German general 18.3 × 15cm (7$\frac{1}{4}$ × 6in) 143
Two Hussars 15.2 × 11.3cm (6 × 4$\frac{1}{2}$in) 144
The Great Kaiser 18.6 × 27.8cm (7$\frac{3}{8}$ × 11in) 145
The Kaiser at ease 23 × 17.7cm (9$\frac{1}{8}$ × 7in) 146
A rude awakening 19.5 × 31cm (7$\frac{3}{4}$ × 12$\frac{1}{4}$in) 147

Fig-leafed Satyr 9.5 × 5.3cm ($3\frac{3}{4} \times 2\frac{1}{8}$in) 148
Fig-leafed Venus 21.8 × 9.8cm ($8\frac{5}{8} \times 3\frac{7}{8}$in) 148
The royal unveiling 18 × 21.8 ($7\frac{1}{8} \times 8\frac{5}{8}$in) 149
War games 13.2 × 18.3cm ($5\frac{1}{4} \times 7\frac{1}{4}$in) 153
'But my pianos play a different tune' 10.1 × 18.3cm ($4 \times 7\frac{1}{4}$in) (Erhardt was a famous French piano manufacturer) 154
'Naked beneath her cloak' 18 × 22.8cm ($7\frac{1}{8} \times 9$in) 156
Cologne cathedral 23 × 19.5cm ($9\frac{1}{8} \times 7\frac{3}{4}$in) 158
Overshadowed by instruments of torture 18.6 × 14.5cm ($7\frac{3}{8} \times 5\frac{3}{4}$in) 160
Balzac 23 × 19.5cm ($9\frac{1}{8} \times 7\frac{3}{4}$in) 161
Balzac – a human prodigy 23 × 18.9 ($9\frac{1}{8} \times 7\frac{1}{2}$in) 163
The death of Balzac (hitherto unpublished) 23 × 18cm ($9\frac{1}{8} \times 7\frac{1}{8}$in) 166
The German hostess 23 × 16.4cm ($9\frac{1}{8} \times 6\frac{1}{2}$in) 169
A native of Alsace 23 × 19.9cm ($9\frac{1}{8} \times 7\frac{5}{8}$in) 171
'We're back in France' 23 × 19.9cm ($9\frac{1}{8} \times 7\frac{5}{8}$in) 173

Select bibliography

Pierre Bonnard

Books documenting *La 628-E8*

Beer, F.J., Pierre Bonnard, Editions Françaises d'Art, 1947
Besson, G., *Bonnard*, Les Editions Braun, 1934
Fermigier, André, *Bonnard*, Edition Cercle d'Art, 1969
Natanson, Thadée, *Le Bonnard que je propose*, Cailler, 1951
Nathanson, Richard, *Bonnard: La 628-E8*, Richard Nathanson, (exh. cat.), 1978
Bonnard, Centre Georges Pompidou, (exh. cat. Phillip's Collection Washington & Dallas Museum of Art), 1984
Rewald, John, *Bonnard*, Museum of Modern Art, New York, (exh. cat.), 1948
Roger-Marx, C., *Pierre Bonnard*, Edition de la Nouvelle Revue Française, 1924
Bonnard Lithographe, André Sauret, 1952
Terrasse, Antoine, *Bonnard*, Skira, 1964
Pierre Bonnard, Gallimard, 1967
Pierre Bonnard, illustrator, Adam Biro, 1988
Terrasse, Charles, *Bonnard*, H. Floury, 1927
Vaillant, *Bonnard*, Thames & Hudson, 1966

Further reading
Bouvet, Francis, *Complete Graphic Works*, Thames and Hudson, 1981
Clair, Jean, *Bonnard*, Henri Screpel, 1975
Cogniat, Raymond, (trans. A. Ross) *Bonnard*, Uffici
Dauberville, Jean and Henry, *L'Oeuvre peint*, Paris, Benheim-Jeune, 4 vols, I – 1888–1905, 1965 – II – 1906–19, 1968, – III 1920–39, 1973 – IV – 1940–7 and supplement 1887–1939, 1974
Fosca, Francois, *Bonnard*, Geneva, Jundig, 1919
Minemura, Toshiaki, *Bonnard*, Tokyo, Shincho Art Library, 1975
Newman, Sasha M., *The Late Paintings*, Thames and Hudson, 1984
Russoli, Franco, *Bonnard*, Paris, Hachette, 1967
Sutton, Denys, *Bonnard*, Faber and Faber, 1957
Terrasse, Michele, *Bonnard at Le Cannet*, Thames and Hudson, 1988

Octave Mirbeau

Novels
La 628-E8, (ed. Juin, H), Union générale d'éditions, 1977
Sébastien Roch
Le Jardin des supplices
Le Journal d'une femme de chambre (Diary of a Chambermaid)
Les Vingt-et-un jours d'un neurasthénique
Farces et Moralites
Contes de la Chaumière
Dingo
L'Abbé Jules
Le Calvaire
La Vache Tachetée
La Pipe de Cidre
Un Gentilhomme

Plays
Les Mauvais Bergers
Les Affaires sont les affaires
Le Foyer
Vieux Ménage
Le Portefeuille

Further reading
Carr, Reg, *Anarchism in France: The Case of Octave Mirbeau*, Manchester University Press, 1966
Schwarz, Martin, *Octave Mirbeau*
Sutton, Denys, 'A Don Juan of Idealism', *Apollo*, Jan. 1987
Wilson, Edmund, 'Octave Mirbeau' *The New Yorker* Apr. 1949